GUARDIANS OF NECESSITY

GUARDIANS OF
NECESSITY

THE ULTIMATE HUMAN
RIGHT + OBLIGATION

SCOTT HATHWAY BARLOW

New York

GUARDIANS OF NECESSITY
THE ULTIMATE HUMAN RIGHT + OBLIGATION

Published in New York, New York, by Morgan James Publishing. Morgan James and The Entrepreneurial Publisher are trademarks of Morgan James, LLC. www.MorganJamesPublishing.com

The Morgan James Speakers Group can bring authors to your live event. For more information or to book an event visit The Morgan James Speakers Group at www.TheMorganJamesSpeakersGroup.com.

A **free** eBook edition is available
with the purchase of this print book.

CLEARLY PRINT YOUR NAME ABOVE IN UPPER CASE

Instructions to claim your free eBook edition:
1. Download the BitLit app for Android or iOS
2. Write your name in **UPPER CASE** on the line
3. Use the BitLit app to submit a photo
4. Download your eBook to any device

ISBN 978-1-63047-602-1 paperback
ISBN 978-1-63047-603-8 eBook
ISBN 978-1-63047-604-5 hardcover
Library of Congress Control Number:
2015935796

Cover Design by:
Ryan Rhodes

Interior Design by:
Bonnie Bushman
The Whole Caboodle Graphic Design

In an effort to support local communities and raise awareness and funds, Morgan James Publishing donates a percentage of all book sales for the life of each book to Habitat for Humanity Peninsula and Greater Williamsburg

Get involved today, visit
www.MorganJamesBuilds.com

Habitat
for Humanity®
Peninsula and
Greater Williamsburg
Building Partner

Thanks To:

Larry Nadeau Baton Rouge Louisiana, for years and years of solid discussion, arguments, partnerships, and most of all friendship.

and...

Kathy Wright Baton Rouge Louisiana, for showing me what dedication really means.

and...

Chuck Mackaline Concord North Carolina, for sharing his common sense, his friendship, and generosity of spirit.

Special Thanks To:

Craig Langwost Preston Maryland, for the thankless job of editing.

Very Special Thanks To:

Rebecca Langwost Barlow Preston Maryland, for being the love of my life, and her constant support during good and bad times.

and...

New York Newsday Managing Editor Alan Hathway, who taught me that you can be successful regardless of the odds, and to never compromise your values. (1906—1977)

and…

Chief Warrant Officer (CW2) Jerome Peter Barlow who was larger than life and never forgotten in death. (6-23-56—7-11-85)

TABLE OF CONTENTS

FOREWORD

In spite of the horrific events splattered all over whatever "screen" we choose to view from, we allow ourselves to be satisfied with the statistics offered that reported violent crimes are down. Or are they? What percentage is acceptable? What is your responsibility or obligation to both yourself and others? These are REAL crimes, happening to REAL people and WE are the REAL solution! **Guardians of Necessity** is a book that speaks to us in a non-partisan, openly honest and enlightening way. Anthropologist Margaret Mead said, *"Never doubt that a small group of thoughtful, committed citizens can change the world. Indeed, it's the only thing that ever has."*

Scott Barlow is an author who has always come to the table of any discussion well read, researched, passionate, and fair on all sides of the topic and this offering is no different. He presents this book from the multiple perspectives of citizen, parent, law enforcer, educator and administrator in political environments. Through this, Scott gives us historical, spiritual, and personal research as food for thought that is both timely and timeless. My husband is fond of saying, *"The truth has a power all its own."* This book has that power.

As a retired law enforcement officer, an Instructor of Self-Defense Instructors who has certified hundreds of self-defense instructors and experts in the field of crime prevention, and a leader in the industry I am constantly searching for material that will expand my base knowledge, and this book has. Whether you are an individual questioning your position of action or inaction, a public safety institution encouraging bystander intervention, a concerned citizen looking for options or a self-defense educator in search of expansion, this book is for you. For it is true, an educated community is an empowered community. Possess it, highlight, underline, reference, bookmark or bend a corner...You'll want to come back to it. This book is your human right and obligation to read for those you care about most.

—Kathy Wright Nadeau
Director of Women's Programming
The R.A.D. Systems of Self-Defense

PREFACE:

I have always felt that my desire to write a book was a bit presumptuous. The older I have become the more I come to understand that the vast majority of what I know has come from reading, while the remaining knowledge has come from personal experience. For this reason I continue to try my hand at writing in the hope that what little knowledge I may possess on this critical topic can be shared and considered a valuable expenditure of the reader's time!

In my 30 plus years of serving in some type of law enforcement capacity I have continually been told by citizens, politicians, attorneys, and human resource folks of the importance of people's rights. We always seem to hear that people have the right not to be abused or bothered by the police, the right to call 911 for any reason and expect police and fire to show up and solve their problems, the right to entitlements from government (from free housing to food stamps), and even have the right to a certain job position and/or promotion.

It is very hard to get too excited about these supposed rights after 30 years of seeing crime victims whose basic human rights were violated. In my black and white world I believe that there is only one "Ultimate Human Right", which is the right of self-defense and the defense of others.

Others have written about "sheep" and "sheepdogs" and used the highly insulting term "sheeple". There have always been and always will be sheep, and sheepdogs, those who need protecting and those willing to do the protecting. Frankly, this has little to do with the government appointing certain folks as sheepdogs and more to do with the inherent willingness to be a protector and prepare to do so successfully.

I trust that the reader already has a bit of this inherent DNA or you would not be interested in this manuscript. You, the reader, are a seeker of knowledge which is the first and most critical step in the preparation to exercise your "ultimate human right". Or, perhaps you are reading this manuscript to scoff at this concept in order to dismiss the author as just one more 2nd Amendment advocate for anarchy and consider government inept.

Nothing could be further from the truth. I hold law enforcement in the highest esteem, but after being an officer for over 30 years I recognize the inherent shortcoming of the profession. Law enforcement is quite good at cleaning up after the fact, but not so much at the preventing of violent crime. My very simple message is that the "ultimate human right" is not only the **only** true right that we as humans have but that we are morally obligated to prepare and to exercise this right!

The 2nd Amendment is just one portion of this manuscript. Regardless of your belief in gun ownership, there clearly can be no argument against the ultimate human right of self-defense and the ultimate human obligation to defend others. I have certainly tried not to focus this entire manuscript on firearms, but as Justice Anthony Scalia put so clearly "the handgun is Americans' preferred weapon of self-defense in part because it can be pointed at a burglar with one hand while the other hand dials the police."

The ultimate human obligation of defending your neighbor **does not stop** after the incident of violence is over. The ultimate human obligation also means you provide emotional support after the fact, and if that means inserting yourself in an uncomfortable position so be it. We may not always be there to prevent the attack or the assault and exercise our ultimate human obligation but we can certainly be there after the fact and provide every bit of support we can, regardless of what personal sacrifice we may think we're making.

As the reader progresses through this manuscript please ask yourself if what we are currently doing as a society to protect and advocate for our fellow humans is enough? I refer back to the adage "it takes a village to raise a child". Regardless of if the reader believes this to be true, we can certainly agree that "it takes a village to protect a child". Let's "turn the page" and move on to a new chapter where the ultimate human right and obligation becomes an important part of our everyday lives!

This manuscript is not presented as a James Michener novel such as "Hawaii" where each and every concept is explored and expounded upon. It is more of a John D. MacDonald novel, direct and to the point with some observations about the human condition.

So read on and feel free to agree or disagree for as my wife tells me, I don't care what the topic is I just love to argue!!

"People who censor books are usually illiterate".
—Travis McGee

CHAPTER ONE

The Ultimate Human Right

The Ultimate Human Right Defined:

First let us discuss what the ultimate human right is not. The ultimate human right does not refer to "rights" as discussed by most folks. It is not about civil rights as enumerated in "The Civil Rights Act of 1964". It is not about Affirmative Action, the Americans with Disabilities Act, the Fair Labor Standards Act, or the 1st Amendment right to free speech and freedom of religion. All very worthy concepts but each pales in comparison to the ultimate human right!

The only absolute human right is the right of self-defense and self-preservation against those who would attempt to injure or kill us and/or those we love. The argument for this right is at the very core of our existence and has been documented in many ways and by many cultures throughout the annals of time.

This is quite a simple theory for many of us but in case this is more difficult for some readers, let's lay the framework for the "ultimate human right". To any, who are students of history both ancient and recent, it is not difficult to find clear support for the ultimate human right. Ancient history and United States history are filled with great thinkers far more eloquent than I. Let's explore some of their thoughts on this topic.

Historical Framework:

The first time I can find this concept discussed is in the bible. I am certainly not a bible scholar but the sixth commandment as discussed in The King James Bible broken down is as follows:

The sixth commandment does not forbid killing in lawful war, *or in our own necessary defense*, nor the magistrate's condemning offenders to death, for those things tend to the preserving of life. The modern interpretation is quite clear. What the sixth commandment forbids is the unjust taking of a legally innocent life. It applies to "murder in cold blood". The bible has always recognized that there are some situations where taking a life is not only permitted but actually warranted.

A more modern, but still quite historical in nature, discussion of the ultimate human right is found in the Magna Carta of 1215. By 1215, thanks to years of unsuccessful foreign policies and heavy taxation demands, England's King John was facing a rebellion by the country's powerful barons. Under duress, he agreed to a charter of liberties known as the Magna Carta (or Great Charter) that would place him and all of England's future sovereigns within a rule of law. This document eventually served as the foundation for the English system of common law. Later generations of Englishmen would celebrate the Magna Carta as a symbol of freedom from oppression, as would the Founding Fathers of the United States of America, who in 1776 looked to the charter as a historical precedent for asserting their liberty from the English crown. While referencing a number of human rights, the Magna Carta puts this concept into words: "No man shall be taken, imprisoned, disseized, outlawed, banished, or in any way *destroyed*."[1]

Moving to more recent history, which is far more relevant to the reader, we will discuss the founding of the United States where we find more specific discussion of the ultimate human right. To further this argument it is important to share with the reader the significant historical sources and thinkers who influenced the crafting of our Declaration of Independence, the Federalist Papers, the Articles of Confederation (First Constitution), the U.S. Constitution, and the Bill of Rights (BOR).

When reviewing the aforementioned documents it is quite apparent that all their respective authors liberally drew from many historical documents.

The bible is clearly an integral part of English common law. Common law is the basis for our current system of statutory law. In England common law coexisted, as civil law did in other countries, with other systems of law. Church courts applied

---

1   Magna Carta of 1215

canon law, urban and rural courts applied local customary law, Chancery and maritime courts applied Roman law. In the seventeenth century common law became the primary source of law, when Parliament established a permanent check on the power of the English king and claimed the right to define the common law and declare other laws subordinate to it.

Scholars such as Thomas Hobbs, John Locke, Jean Jacques Rousseau discussed concepts such as legitimacy of leader, social contract theory, divine right, and the consent of governed. They were the great thinkers of their times. Thomas Jefferson, who authored the Declaration of Independence, was a great reader of these and other scholars. James Monroe, Alexander Hamilton, and John Jay, the three primary writers of the federalist papers, were also great readers of these and other scholars.

The Social Contract Theory:

When reading the works of these scholars, in particular the social contract theory, the concept of citizens consent to be governed by a just government stands out. If at any time the citizens decide they do not wish to be governed by the current form of government, because of tyranny and human rights violations they have an absolute right to armed rebellion. This clearly is a significant form of the ultimate human right and obligation.[2]

The Declaration of Independence:

The Declaration of Independence was authored by one of the great thinkers of his time, Thomas Jefferson. Thomas Jefferson

---

2   Locke, John. The Social Contract Theory.

made no claim to all of his concepts and readily admitted to liberally drawing from history and history's great writers. "We hold these truths to be self-evident, that all men are created equal, that they are endowed by their Creator with certain unalienable Rights that among these are *Life, Liberty and the pursuit of Happiness.*"[3]

"That to secure these rights, Governments are instituted among Men, deriving their just powers from the consent of the governed, That whenever any Form of Government becomes destructive of these ends, it is the Right of the People to alter or to abolish it, and to institute new Government, laying its foundation on such principles and organizing its powers in such form, as to them shall seem most likely to affect their Safety and Happiness".

When reading this passage it is simple to see that Jefferson incorporated much of the same conceptual thinking as was found in the social contract theory.

Our constitution was ratified based on two significant documents, the federalist papers and the BOR. The federalist papers were written to advocate and educate people on the importance of ratifying our constitution. The BOR was written to protect all people's civil liberties. Civil liberties are protections that individuals have from the government, and specify what government cannot do.

The Federalist Papers:
The federalist papers were authored by James Monroe, Alexander Hamilton, and John Jay. They were written to advocate for the

---

3   Jefferson, Thomas. The Declaration of Independence.

ratification of our constitution. When we read many of these 87 articles we can see much similarity with the great thinkers who advocated for the social contract theory.

The federalist papers were described by Thomas Jefferson as "The best commentary on the principles of government ever written".

The Bill of Rights:

The BOR was considered so critical to the formation of the new democratic republic that several of the original thirteen states refused to ratify the constitution until the BOR was incorporated as the first ten amendments to the constitution! Historians are in agreement that if not for the BOR, and the federalist papers, the articles of confederation (our first constitution) would not have been replaced with our current constitution.

The Bill of Rights 5th Amendment:

The BOR 5th Amendment states "No person shall be deprived **of life liberty** or property without due process of law". In more simple terms no one can legally take a life other than the government after due process. This clearly supports the ultimate human right of self-defense in that human life is considered so sacred that our constitution ensured that we had protections requiring a system of due process prior to any punishment up to and including capital punishment.

No predator has the right to injure or kill another. Our absolute right to self-defense follows in line with this concept.

The Bill of Rights 2ⁿᵈ Amendment:

To ensure that the people were able to exercise the ***Ultimate Human Right of Self Defense*** the second amendment was written in to the BOR. The BOR 2ⁿᵈ Amendment states "A well-regulated Militia, being necessary to the security of a free State, ***the right of the people to keep and bear Arms***, shall not be infringed".

There are still many arguments as to the intent of the 2nd Amendment though it seems quite clear that it was put in place out of fear of an oppressive government. Self-defense is the logical next step in the equation to not only defend against an oppressive government but to be able to defend against a violent attack.

Civil Rights Amendments:

Additional amend ments to the constitution such as the 13th, 14th, 15th, 19th, and 26th amendments require the government to protect its citizens. These protections are known as civil rights. The first ten amendments are known as civil liberties. The differences between these are explained as follows: civil rights are where the government protects its citizens, and civil liberties are protections against the government.

Accountability:

I have laid some historical framework for the ultimate human right and now it is time to discuss who, or what body, holds the responsibility for this right of defense. Many would argue that it is the government's responsibility to provide it's citizenry with these protections by forming a military, federal law enforcement, state police, and local police.

This clearly is a valid argument. As this is my "world", so to speak, let's talk about what federal, state, and local government realistically can and cannot do. In order to best discuss our government's obligations and abilities we should first discuss government itself.

There are many different forms of government and political systems that dictate how power is distributed among leaders and citizens. Authoritarian systems give ultimate power to the state while non-authoritarian systems, like democracy, place power largely in the hands of the people.

Democracy is based on the principle of popular sovereignty, giving the people the ultimate power to govern. The meaning of citizenship is key to the definition of democracy, where citizens are believed to have rights protecting them from government as well as responsibilities the government has to its citizens.

I think we can agree that the United States is a non-authoritarian form of government, a democracy. I think we can also agree that we have no desire to live in an authoritarian form of government.

> *"Those who give up essential liberty to obtain a little temporary safety, deserve neither liberty nor safety".*
> **—Ben Franklin**

> *"If all that Americans want is security, they can go to prison. They'll have enough to eat, a bed and roof over their head".*
> **—Dwight Eisenhower**

Democracy becomes the clear choice when compared to other forms of government. There are many different forms of democracy, with subtle but important differences.

Anarchy:

An argument can even be made that Anarchy can be considered a form of democracy though a totally ineffective one since by definition it is the absence of government and rules. But it truly is the ultimate freedom, for the strongest and most ruthless.

Elite Democracy:

An elite democracy is one where citizens have limited choices, and choose among elite competing leaders. We, in the U.S., may be headed in this direction with our current ineffective two party system but we are not there yet.

Pure Democracy:

A pure democracy, in theory, is one where the citizens ultimately have control of their lives. All decisions of government are put to a vote. This is also known as a direct democracy, or a true democracy. It is a system whereby citizens vote directly on issues as opposed to electing representatives to vote for them. We still use this philosophy for certain referendums that our elected representatives' want input on. This form of democracy is quite unwieldy in a county with a large population.

Democratic Republic:

The democracy our founders chose is one called a democratic republic. In a democratic republic we, the citizens, choose our representatives to make decisions for us. This is a democracy that will succeed or fail based on the willingness of the citizens to take the election process seriously. Citizens who are informed and willing to vote and hold their representatives accountable are critical to the success of this "grand experiment".

To make this even more complicated there are two primary arguments on how our government, a representative democracy, functions. Should our government provide procedural guarantees or substantive guarantees?

In a **Procedural** form of democracy there is a set of normative principles for democratic decision making. A more simplistic definition is a form of democracy used in a capitalistic economy where the government guarantees, or tries to maintain, an even playing field for all.

In a **Substantive** form of democracy there are far more government guarantees such as the requirement that a democratic government **must** guarantee civil rights and liberties. To take this a step further we could add social and economic rights to the list of substantive outcomes a democracy ensures. Again, a simplistic definition is a form of democracy used in a socialist economy where the government guarantees equal outcomes for all its citizens.

It is clear that procedural and substantive views of democracy are at odds with each other. It is also clear that our government incorporates a bit of both of these philosophies, though currently with leanings more toward the procedural arena.

The question to the reader is who are you? Do you believe that the government is responsible for your well-being, success, and overall life? Or…do you believe it is the government's job to provide an equal playing field and the end result is based on your hard work, preparation, and yes a bit of luck and good fortune?

If you, the reader, wish to sit back and expect our government to be responsible for everything in your life, you have no need to prepare and you should ignore the rest of this book. If you believe that the government may do its best but your ultimate result is based on your own efforts, read on and prepare to pick up where the government leaves off.

Policing in a Democratic (free) Society:
The reality of this is that the police have significant limitations. Police are quite good at showing up after the fact and cleaning up by investigating, arresting, and prosecuting utilizing the criminal justice system. This being said, police are not nearly as good at preventing crime. This leaves crime victims at a significant disadvantage.

Yes, reported violent crime has seen a statistical decrease. Is this due to better policing or just the natural ebb and flow of crime? I will leave this up to the reader to decide, though I have my own strong opinions.

According to the FBI, statistically, numbers indicate that murders declined 6.9 percent, forcible rapes declined 10.6 percent, aggravated assaults decreased 6.6 percent and robbery offenses decreased 1.8 percent from 2012. In addition the data reportedly indicates that burglary offenses decreased 8.1 percent, larceny-theft offenses decreased 4.7 percent and motor vehicle thefts decreased by 3.2 percent from 2012. These statistics are based upon data collected during the first six months of 2013 submitted by nearly 13,000 federal and state law enforcement agencies around the nation.

This seems pretty significant unless you are one of the crime victims, whereupon you probably do not care that violent crime is on a downward trend. Statistics can be manipulated, and presented in many differing formats where the same numbers tell very different stories. The old adage that there are "lies, damn lies, and statistics" is quite telling. My experience is that police agencies love to take credit for crime stats when they decrease but are very quiet when they increase.

It seems quite simple to me; take responsibility for the safety and well-being of you and those you care about. Be a sheepdog, a protector for your family and friends. For the younger reader this may seem simple. You are thinking; I am young, strong, fast, and well trained. In other words a lean mean fighting machine. In reality a credo to live by is; there is always someone stronger and better trained then you, or in some cases multiple someones!

As I have grown older I look back and realize I was not quite as well-equipped as I thought I was in "the day". As the reader may have guessed I am an advocate for what engineers call a "mechanical advantage". A mechanical advantage is simply utilizing a tool whenever possible. If your hand is not strong enough to turn a bolt, use a wrench; if your body weight is not heavy enough to lift a load; use a lever.

So, are you convinced? Are you willing to take responsibility for your ultimate human right? Do you recognize that even though the government is responsible to provide safeguards for you and your loved ones, we live in a form of government that allows for great freedoms and thus many risks to allow for these freedoms? Do you recognize that no matter how many police the government provides they cannot be, and you do not want them to be, everywhere?

Read on, and prepare to take responsibility for your own safety and that of those you care for!

The theory of Single ignorance v. double ignorance: "Is distinguishing between simple ignorance, the mere lack of knowledge, and double ignorance, the absence of knowledge coupled with the delusion of having genuine knowledge. Thus to be singly ignorant you must only accept that you do not know."

—Plato

"Tact is the ability to tell someone to go to hell in such a way that they look forward to the trip".

—Winston Churchill

CHAPTER TWO

THE ULTIMATE HUMAN OBLIGATION

The Ultimate Human Obligation Defined:

Is obligation too strong a term? I think not! In a world where violence is so prevalent can we truly expect to stand by and allow predators to stalk, injure, and kill our fellow humans? In the era of the bystander with the cell phone video recording attack after attack and taking no action, this argument must be made.

I intend to make the case for a moral and ethical obligation for all of us to be "sheepdogs" (protectors of our fellow humans). As the reader progresses through this chapter, the definition of being a protector will become clearer. Being a protector of our fellow human beings is not just the physical aspect of coming to a person's aid when they are in need, it also involves sounding the alarm by calling for help, acting as a witness if called upon, and providing emotional support after the fact.

The choice of self-defense or the defense of others may seem to the novice as a choice, where in reality many times it is not. J R.R. Tolkien's fictional character "Eowyn" summed up this concept beautifully:

> *"The women of this country learned long ago, those without swords can still die upon them".*
> —**Eowyn**

I begin this chapter with some case studies that the reader may find hard to believe, I certainly did.

Case Examples (Failure to Render Aid):

Kitty Genovese—On March 13, 1964 Genovese, 28 years old, was on her way back to her Queens, New York, apartment from work at 3am when she was stabbed to death by a serial rapist and murderer. According to newspaper accounts, the attack lasted for at least a half an hour during which time Genovese screamed and pleaded for help. The murderer attacked Genovese and stabbed her, then fled the scene after attracting the attention of a neighbor. The killer then returned ten minutes later and finished the assault. Newspaper reports after Genovese's death claimed that 38 witnesses watched the stabbings and failed to intervene or even contact the police until after the attacker fled and Genovese had died.

Axel Casian—On June 16, 2008, on a country road outside Turlock, California, friends, family and strangers, including a volunteer fire chief, stood by as Sergio Aguiar methodically stomped his two-year-old son Axel Casian to death, explaining in a calm voice that he "had to get the demons out" of the boy. He stopped at one point to turn on the hazard lights on his truck. No one moved to take the child or attack Aguiar.

Witnesses said they were all afraid to intervene because Aguiar "might have something in his pocket", although some people looked for rocks or boards hoping to find something to subdue him.

Esmin Green—In June of 2008 49-year-old Esmin Green collapsed in the waiting room of Kings County Hospital Center in Brooklyn after waiting nearly 24 hours for treatment. She was ignored by other people present in the room and two security guards. She was helped after an hour passed but died.

Hugo Alfredo Tale-Yax—In April of 2010 Hugo Alfredo Tale-Yax was stabbed to death in New York City after coming to the aid of a woman who was being attacked by a robber. Yax was on the sidewalk for more than an hour before firefighters arrived. Almost twenty-five people walked by while he lay dying on a sidewalk in Queens, several stared at Yax, one of them took pictures; however, none of them helped or called emergency services.

Wang Yue—In October of 2011, a two-year-old girl, Wang Yue, was hit by a small, white van in the city of Foshan, China, then run over by a large truck when she was not moved by bystanders. A total of 18 people ignored her, some going so far as to walk around the blood. The girl was left for 7 minutes before a recycler, Chen Xianmei, picked up the toddler and called for help. The child died eight days later.

Thomas A. Moehlman—According to St. Louis County police, the incident occurred when the victim was purchasing his ticket at an automated kiosk. A suspect grabbed the victim's money as he attempted to purchase a ticket. When the victim held tight to the cash, the suspect struck him in the face and ran off with $22.

Randy Moehlman, the victim's son, tells Daily RFT that his father was recently diagnosed with Parkinson's disease. Still, he remains active and frequently uses MetroLink to journey out for lunch. Moehlman says his father was doing just that last Tuesday when he was mugged and assaulted at the MetroLink stop.

"There were at least a half-dozen other commuters on the platform who saw this and heard my dad's screams," says Moehlman. "But they just chose to ignore him, and my father being deaf can't call the police himself." Help arrived only after a woman getting off a train noticed Moehlman's bloody father and dialed 911. But since she had not witnessed the robbery, she was unable to offer police assistance.

Randy Moehlman, the son, of a 69-year-old deaf man robbed and assaulted last week at a MetroLink platform isn't sure which is worse: that there was no security around to prevent his father from being mugged in broad daylight or that bystanders at the Richmond Heights' station ignored his father's pleas following the attack.

Allen Haywood—In Washington D.C. Allen Haywood was randomly and viciously attacked by two kids on the platform of the L'Enfant Plaza Metro station. Dozens of people witnessed it. Several people filmed it. Nobody helped.

As seen in the video, Haywood repeatedly asked the girl why she was attacking him, pleading with her to end it. "Stop it! Stop it! Goddamn it! You stop this shit right now! I did nothing to you!"

Haywood looked to strangers for help, but all he saw were other kids with their cell phones out, recording the scene and laughing.

"I can understand people not wanting to get physically involved," says Haywood, who's 47 and works in a Friendship Heights flower shop. "But nobody pressed the emergency button or went to the booth," as far as he knows.

Each of these incidents was reported in the print media and are simple to find with a basic search engine. It is not difficult to find many of these cases and there is significant research explaining bystander's lack of actions. The common term seems to be "bystander apathy". As a simple cop, I have simple analysis. This lack of willingness to accept the ultimate human obligation is lack of courage, lack of empathy, and a lack of a moral compass.

Bystander Apathy:

In the early 1980s Researchers Darley and Latane explained a bystander's lack of willingness to assist with a theory of bystander intervention called the 'arousal cost-reward model'. This model illustrates that bystanders intervene most when they perceive the personal costs of helping to be low and the costs of not helping are perceived as being high.[4]

Other social psychologists have expanded these conclusions to explain other social phenomena. In 1994, social psychologists Christy and Voigt sought a better understanding of the lack of bystander intervention in episodes of public child abuse. They surveyed 269 witnesses who stated that they had seen instances of child abuse. While roughly half of the participants in the survey stated that these instances occurred in public, only one out of four witnesses acted to intervene. [5]

This research led to the conclusion that bystander intervention in situations like child abuse is most likely to occur when the bystander is able to mentally produce a number of feasible solutions or strategies to end the perceived conflict.

Additionally, Christy and Voigt found that bystanders are more likely to intervene when they have a relationship with the victim or can identify with the victim in some way. As more studies are made that examine what specifically increases the likelihood of bystander intervention, social psychologists have begun making suggestions on how to expand the bystander effect to improve rape prevention education programs and to analyze the existence of the bystander effect in children by studying bullying.

Police officers and psychologists have explained the inaction of bystanders as justified in that "ordinary people aren't going

---

4   Latane, B & Darley, J. Bystander Apathy, 1969.
5   Christy, Cathryn A & Voigt, Harrison. Bystander Responses to Public Episodes of Child Abuse. July 2006.

to tackle a psychotic," that they were not "psychologically prepared" to intervene, and that being frozen in indecision and fear is a normal reaction.

Bystander Training:

Studies have also shown that the result of bystander intervention is the reduced likelihood of violent attempts being successful, the reduction of overall violence, and increased intervention by others in conflict situations. For these reasons, anti-bystander apathy education programs have been implemented by a number of different institutions to increase helping behavior, especially in situations of sexual violence or violence against children.

There has been some action by government to include laws that hold bystanders responsible when they witness an emergency.

The Charter of Human Rights and Freedoms of Quebec makes it mandatory to "come to the aid of anyone whose life is in peril, either personally or calling for aid, unless it involves danger to himself or a third person, or he has another valid reason". It is therefore a legal obligation to assist people in Quebec.[6]

The Brazilian Penal Code states that it is a crime not to rescue (or call emergency services when appropriate) injured or disabled people, including those found under grave and imminent danger, as long as it safe to do so. This also includes abandoned children.[7]

---

6   Charter of Human Rights and Freedomes. Civil Code of Quebec.
7   Brazilian Penal Code. Abandonment of Children.

In the USA, Good Samaritan laws have been implemented to protect bystanders who acted in good faith. Many organizations are including bystander training. For example, the United States Department of the Army is doing bystander training with respect to sexual assault. Some organizations routinely do bystander training with respect to safety issues. Others have been doing bystander training with respect to diversity issues. Many universities are also using bystander research to improve bystander attitudes in cases of rape.[8]

Do we need to explore this concept further? I suppose so. As discussed in the previous chapter there is a long history of the ultimate human right being discussed and advocated. In this chapter I propose that it is truly one step more, the ultimate human obligation!

Case Study (A Case of Multiple Errors):

I recently read about a case where a college student (Jesse Matthew Jr) was dismissed from one university for sexual assault (rape). This same student turned up at a second university and was again dismissed for a sexual assault. No actions were taken through the criminal justice system in either case.

This former student, many years later, has been linked to two deaths of college students through DNA. Unfortunately serial cases are more prevalent than many would like to accept. Arrest and prosecution is really the only way that people who prey on others are truly stopped. Without arrest and prosecution the serial criminal just moves on to different places where it is even more difficult to track them.

---

8   Good Samaritan Laws. Wikipedia.

In this particular case, as with many others, there are several questions that need to be addressed.

- Did each university provide the first two victims with the tools (prevention and awareness) to prevent these attacks?
- Did each university provide the first two victims with appropriate support to defend themselves (after the event follow-up) and others by utilizing the legal process?
- What did the suspect learn from the actions, or inactions, of the university and his first two victims?

The first question is a simple one. All college students should receive basic education of how to avoid being a crime victim, what programs are available at the university, and what policies and processes are in place if victimization occurs. If these issues were not addressed, shame on the universities.

In response to the second question, I do not advocate for victims being pressured to prosecute their aggressors (suspects). This is a very personal decision that must be made by the victim(s) themselves. I do advocate for universities, as well as local, state, and federal government to be staunch advocates for victims so they are willing to prosecute. I have not seen adequate efforts put forth in this venue. We have come a long way with victim advocates but we have a long way to go. Many schools do not wish the negative publicity that comes with serious violent crimes and government is quite cold and impersonal with violent crime victims.

But....what would have happened if the first sexual assault victim had felt staunch support and decided to utilize the criminal justice system to defend herself and others? Would there have been a second sexual assault victim? Would there be two dead victims, or more, by this same offender?

In response to the third, and most unsettling, question: what did the offender (and other offenders) learn from this scenario? The answer is quite simple and quite chilling. Leave no witnesses to the crime. Clearly this offender received punishment (expulsion) based on the victims (witnesses) coming forward. If there are no witnesses to the crime there will be no punishment, hence a minimum result of two dead victims.

The trend is quite clear. Prey on the sheep and do not allow the sheepdogs to find you by leaving no witnesses. This in no way is an isolated incident. It is becoming more and more common to kill and dispose of the victims of violent crime in order to thwart the investigation which is so reliant on forensic DNA evidence.

The Ultimate Obligation Framework (History and The Five Great Religions):

History shows a very specific pattern that supports this ultimate obligation. In the first chapter we established that citizens of this country require a form of democracy, and a democracy requires citizens to take responsibility for *Life, Liberty and the pursuit of Happiness*. It is then fitting to look back to our first known democracy.

Athens, Greece:

As the world's first known democracy, Athenians were compelled to fight for their new democracy. Before the birth of Christ, the Athenian military was exceptionally successful and many historians attribute this success to the Athenian political system. An excellent example of this success was the Athenian victory over a superior Persian force at Marathon in 490 B.C.

On numerous subsequent occasions, Athenian citizens were called upon to go into battle against other states, both Greek and foreign. Athens had a small standing army and navy as the majority of Athenians were civilians with family requirements as merchants and farmers. The Athenian military can be compared to the American National Guard of citizen soldiers.

In fact, the largest component of the army was the infantry composed of *hoplites*, citizens fighting in a full set of armor. They went into battle protected by a helmet, breastplate, and greaves (shin guards), carrying a large round shield and long thrusting spear. On occasion, the state would issue such equipment to citizens who could not afford a set of their own, though in most cases the citizen soldier was required to provide their own tools of war, which in many cases were passed down from father to son.

An Athenian was required to provide two years' service during which time they were exempt from all taxes. Upon the completion of these two years the citizen soldier was granted full citizenship. Richer Athenians, who could provide their own mount, enrolled in the cavalry, a smaller elite military force made up of those wealthy enough to own and maintain a good mount.

Hence, not only was democracy born, but also the clear ultimate obligation to provide protection and defense of family and homeland.[9]

Religious Faith (The Five Great Religions):

While serving as a chief of police I still vividly remember attending meetings with merchants who were upset about the homeless population in the downtown shopping district. They, along with some council members, felt during the shopping season, in particular Christmas it sent a bad image to have multiple homeless persons in the area. In reality, there is little that the police can do in relation to the homeless. It is not against the law to be homeless and there are fewer and fewer resources available to provide services for the homeless.

I quickly learned the value of local churches that all stepped up and took turns providing shelter for the homeless during the cold months. Had this had not occurred there would have been nothing I could have done to assist. I hold pastors, priests, rabbis, and preachers in very high esteem. I believe that religion, for all its faults and human error, is a huge benefit to society. Religion in many ways leads the way when it comes to the ultimate human obligation of protecting others.

Although I consider myself quite spiritual I spend little time practicing any particular faith. I do believe that a spiritual argument can be made for the ultimate human obligation of self-defense and the defense of others. Most would agree that there are five major religious faiths in the

---

9   Athenian Military. Wikipedia.

world. If we take a few moments to explore each of these religions there is a clear argument for ultimate human right and obligation in each.

> *"To me organized religion, the formalities and routines, is like being marched in formation to look at the sunset".*
> —**John D. MacDonald**

Judaism: The Faith:

Judaism began about 4000 years ago with the Hebrew people in the Middle East. Abraham is considered the father of Judaism, because he promoted the central idea of the Jewish faith: that there is one God. At the time people in the Middle East worshipped many gods. It is said that Abraham and his wife Sarah, who were old and childless, were told by God that "their children would be as plentiful as the stars in the sky and that they would live in a land of their own, the Promised Land". This gradually came true.

Abraham's son, Isaac in turn had a son, Jacob, also called Israel. In this way the descendants of Abraham came to be known as the Israelites. God promised the Israelites he would care for them as long as they obeyed God's laws. For a time the Hebrews lived in Egypt where they were enslaved. Moses, a Hebrew, was chosen by God to lead. Moses led the Hebrew people out of Egypt and through the Sinai Desert toward the Promised Land. At Mt. Sinai, God gave Moses the laws which would guide the Israelites to this day. The laws are called the

Ten Commandments and form the basis of the Torah, the book of Jewish law.

Judaism Argument for the Ultimate Human Right:

Rabbi Aryeh's Interpretation of the Torah:

"We fight because self-defense is a mandate from the Bible, the Torah, called by many the Old Testament. We fight to defend life. Because life is precious, the ultimate, we must defend it. The very definition of self-defense is permission to kill the one who is coming toward you to kill you. Self-defense is not simply our right to pray or support with words, but do whatever is needed to stay alive and protect our families."

"A war to defend and stop those coming to kill you is a moral war. It is called a Just War. And we defend not only ourselves, we defend others. The Bible, the Torah that is, says, 'Do not stand idly by while the blood of our brother is being spilled'. We also have permission to kill those coming to rape a woman. The Bible, Old Testament, tells us so in Exodus. It is our obligation."[10]

Christianity: The Faith:

Christians believe in a loving God who has revealed himself and can be known in a personal way, in this life. With Jesus Christ, the person's focus is not on religious rituals or performing good works, but on enjoying a relationship with God and growing to know him better.

---

10 Spero, Aryeh. Self Defense is a Religious Obligation. American Thinker. August 22, 2014.

Faith in Jesus Christ himself, not just in his teachings, is how the Christian experiences joy and a meaningful life. In his life on Earth, Jesus did not identify himself as a prophet pointing to God or as a teacher of enlightenment. Rather, Jesus claimed to be God in human form. He performed miracles, forgave people of their sin and said that anyone who believed in him would have eternal life. Christians regard the Bible as God's written message to humankind. In addition to being an historical record of Jesus' life and miracles, the Bible reveals God's personality, his love and truth, and how one can have a relationship with him.

Whatever circumstances a Christian is dealing with in their life, the Bible teaches that they can confidently turn to a wise and powerful God who genuinely loves them. They believe that God answers prayer and that life takes on meaning as they live to honor him.

Christian Argument for the Ultimate Human Right:
Theodore Beza the Protestant Reformer (1519-1605):

"Hence it comes about that the man who meets with highway robbers, by whom no one is murdered without the consent of the will of God, has the power in accordance with the authority of the laws to resist them in just self-defense which incurs no blame because no one forsooth has (received) a special command from God that he meekly allow himself to be slain by robbers".

Theodore Beza felt that God laid the expectation of self-defense at the feet of heads of families that they protect, provide for and defend their families and protect and defend their countries. "Little ones cannot do so, and rely solely on those who bore them. God no more loves the willing neglect of their safety than He loves child abuse. He no more appreciates the willingness to ignore the sanctity of our own lives than He approves of the abuse of our own bodies and souls. God hasn't called us to save the society by sacrificing our children or ourselves to robbers, home invaders, rapists or murderers".[11]

Self-defense may actually result in one of the great examples of human love. Christ Himself said, "Greater love has no one than this that he lay down his life for his friends." (John 15:14).

Islam: The Faith:

Muslims believe there is the one almighty God, named Allah, who is infinitely superior to and transcendent from humankind. Allah is viewed as the creator of the universe and the source of all good and all evil. Everything that happens is Allah's will. He is a powerful and strict judge, who will be merciful toward followers depending on the sufficiency of their life's good works and religious devotion. A follower's relationship with Allah is as a servant to Allah.

Though a Muslim honors several prophets, Muhammad is considered the last prophet and his words and lifestyle are that person's authority. For many people, Islam matches their expectations about religion and deity. Islam teaches that there is one supreme God, who is worshiped through good deeds and disciplined religious rituals. After death a person is rewarded or punished according to their religious devotion.

---

11   Beza, Thodore. Christians, The 2nd Amendment and the Duty of Self Defense. Smith, Herschel.

Muslims believe that giving up one's life for Allah is a sure way of entering Paradise.

Islamic Argument for the Ultimate Human Right:

Ram Puniyani, a scholar in Islamic studies argues:

"Islam does not condone violence but, like other religions, does believe in self-defense".[12]

Mark Juergensmeyer, another Islamic scholar argues:

"Like all religions, Islam occasionally allows for force while stressing that the main spiritual goal is one of nonviolence and peace. Although it would be a mistake to think that Islam is inherently a violent religion, it would be equally inappropriate to fail to understand the conditions under which believers might feel justified in acting violently against those whom their tradition feels should be opposed".[13]

Chandra Muzaffar, an Islamic scholar explains:

"Exposition on resisting aggression, oppression and injustice lays down the parameters within which fighting or the use of violence is legitimate. What this means is that one can use the Quran as the criterion for when violence is legitimate and when it is not".[14]

Hinduism: The Faith:

Most Hindus worship one being of ultimate oneness (Brahman) through infinite representations of gods and goddesses. These various manifestations of gods and goddesses become incarnate within idols, temples, gurus, rivers, animals.

12   Puniyani, Ram. Understanding the Prophet Mohammad and Islam.
13   Juergensmeyer, Mark. Islamic Views on Violence. Wikipedia.
14   Muzaffar, Chandra. Interview on Frontline.

Hindus believe their position in this present life was determined by their actions in a previous life. Hinduism therefore provides a possible explanation for suffering and evil in this life. If a person's behavior before was evil, they might justifiably experience tremendous hardships in this life. Pain, disease, poverty or a disaster like a flood is deserved by that person because of their own evil actions, usually from a previous lifetime.

A Hindu's goal is to become free from the law of karma... to be free from continuous reincarnations. Only the soul matters which will one day be free of the cycle of rebirths and be at rest.

Hinduism Argument for the Ultimate Human Right:

Hindus' believe in the concept of Ahimsa which means kindness and non-violence towards all living things including animals; it respects living beings as a unity, the belief that all living things are not just connected but integrally part of each other. Indian leader Mahatma Gandhi strongly believed in this principle and based his resistance to British rule in India and his campaign for Indian Independence on Ahimsa. Avoidance of verbal and physical violence is also a part of this principle, although ahimsa recognizes the need for self-defense when necessary, as a sign of a strong spirit. Ahimsa is closely connected with the notion that all kinds of violence will result in negative karmic consequences.

Hindus believe that violence in self-defense can be justified, and they consider a soldier who kills enemies in combat as performing a legitimate duty.

Buddhism:

Buddhists do not worship any gods or God. People outside of Buddhism often think that Buddhists worship the Buddha. However, the Buddha (Siddhartha Gautama) never claimed to be divine, but rather he is viewed by Buddhists as having attained what they are also striving to attain, which is spiritual enlightenment and, with it, freedom from the continuous cycle of life and death. Most Buddhists believe a person has countless rebirths, which inevitably include suffering. A Buddhist seeks to end these rebirths. Buddhists believe it is a person's cravings, aversion and delusion that cause these rebirths. Therefore, the goal of a Buddhist is to purify one's heart and to let go of all yearnings toward sensual desires and the attachment to oneself.

Buddhists follow a list of religious principles and very dedicated meditation. When a Buddhist meditates it is not the same as praying or focusing on a god, it is more of self-discipline. Through practiced meditation a person may reach Nirvana.

Buddhism's Argument for the Ultimate Human Right:

Buddhism, unlike Hinduism, has strong misgivings about violent ways of punishing criminals and about war. Both were not explicitly condemned, but peaceful ways of conflict resolution and punishment with the least amount of injury were encouraged. The early texts condemn the mental states that lead to violent behavior.

The five major religions of the world, some more strongly that others, all make a case for the ultimate human right of self-defense, and the ultimate human obligation to defend others.

"Before becoming a Muslim, a Sikh, a Hindu, a Buddhist, a Jew, or a Christian become a Human first".
    —Unknown

Accountability for the Ultimate Human Obligation:
How strongly does the reader feel about our obligation to defend ourselves and others with all means necessary? Who is responsible for the defense? Should we just advocate for compliance in hopes that the violent criminal will not maim or kill their victim(s)?

I am not making light of the complexity of these questions. I feel strongly that we have a moral obligation to defend ourselves and others in direct relation to our preparation and abilities. If we fail to prepare then we have failed in our moral obligation.

I am not an advocate for training children to be defenders. I am not referring to bullying, where the stakes are not nearly as high. There are totally differing tactics and techniques for dealing with the bully. I am speaking in reference to violent crimes. Theodore Beza is correct when he stated "Little ones cannot do so, and rely solely on those who bore them".

The ultimate responsibility for self-defense rests with the adult. Educating children and providing age based and maturity based information is excellent. What I do not recommend is frightening children to the extent that they live their lives in constant fear. It is up to the adult parent to determine how much information they provide to their children and hopefully maintain a healthy balance.

It is quite clear to me that compliance does not guarantee safety for the victim and certainly not for future victims. It is also quite clear to me that compliance in some cases is an option, though I would prefer to use the term "tactical compliance". Simply put, compliance though a choice based on the circumstances, should be switched to defending quickly and mercilessly if circumstances change and become more advantageous to the person under attack.

> *"Don't hit at all if it is honorably possible to avoid hitting; but never hit soft".*
> **—Theodore Roosevelt**

I am aware that there are many conflicting opinions for this theory but I reserve the right to choose the philosophy that best supports what I believe is a clear moral obligation of self-defense and defense of others. The historical perspective is overwhelmingly in support of not only the ultimate right, but the ultimate obligation as well.

What should concern many of us is the lack of empathy that seems so prevalent in our current society. It seems incredible to me that so many will immediately begin recording a violent attack but will make no attempt to stop said attack by exercising their ultimate human obligation.

New Jersey—In New Jersey a young mother was shown in a cell phone video being pummeled by a former co-worker. Although many witness videoed the attack only the mother's 2-year-old son came to her rescue.

Catherine Ferreira, 27, suffered a broken nose and a mild concussion at the hands of Latia Harris, 25, who was captured on video throwing the petite woman to the ground like a rag doll and repeatedly punching her in the face.

California—In California on October 24, 2009, in Richmond, a city on the northeast side of the San Francisco Bay in California, U.S., a 15-year-old female student of Richmond High School was gang raped repeatedly by a group of young males in a courtyard on the school campus while a homecoming dance was being held in the gymnasium.

This incident received national attention based on the fact that as many as 20 witnesses are believed to have been aware of the attack, but for more than two hours no one notified the police, or attempted to stop the attack.

These are some of the more obscene examples of the lack of a moral compass and the unwillingness of our fellow humans to exercise the ultimate human obligation! Take a few minutes to peruse the World Wide Web and you can find many, many more. Can there really be any argument that the right and obligation truly do exist? Can there be any real justification for the able bodied to not help defend others against an attack, and that those not able bodied should at least sound the alarm? Does it take a two year old child protecting his mother to teach us what should be done?

"In all emotional and moral conflicts the thing you find most difficult to do is normally what you should do".
—Meyer

CHAPTER THREE

THE LEGAL CLIMATE

The legal climate seems quite liberal when it comes to cases of self-defense, particularly in the home. Where we seem to cross the line is when there is mutual combat, with no clear primary aggressor or when there was a clear path to retreat to avoid using high levels of force. There have been many significant cases that received extreme levels of public scrutiny. I will explore one of the most recent ones.

Self-Defense (?):

One of the most high profile cases is a poor illustration of the right to self-defense, but it is quite telling as it relates to current public opinion. The Trayvon Martin killing by the over committed self-appointed watch captain should give us a pretty clear picture of how liberal the legal climate is. It is pretty simplistic when a citizen is defending himself or others from significant injury or death, but not so clear when the confrontation is initiated by the one who ends up in a self-defense mode.

There are arguments to be made on both sides of the issue in relation to George Zimmerman. Evidence and recreating the event showed that Mr. Zimmerman was frustrated at the level of property crime in his neighborhood, and the inability of law enforcement to respond quickly enough, Mr. Zimmerman decided to follow Mr. Martin, whom he felt did not belong in his neighborhood and seemed suspicious in nature.

Mr. Martin was apparently unhappy with being followed and a confrontation ensued. It is not clear who initiated the confrontation as the only eye witness we have is Mr. Zimmerman. Based on injuries and forensics it is also quite clear that Mr. Zimmerman was losing the physical confrontation. Mr. Zimmerman chose to carry and use his firearm in what he claimed was self-defense.

In support of Mr. Martin the manner of Mr. Zimmerman's approach could have been perceived as threatening.

In support of Mr. Zimmerman, no one has the right to severely beat another just because they do not like the manner of the person approaching.

It is also quite important to note that a jury of Mr. Zimmerman's peers did not find him innocent. They, as the law requires, found that there was not enough evidence to prove guilt beyond a reasonable doubt!

I will not pass judgment on this case, but I will share what 30 years of policing has taught me. If you wish to become involved in the apprehension of potential offenders without the benefits of the standard protections police have such as; **backup**, radio communication, **backup**, Tasers, **backup**, chemical weapons, **backup**, training, **backup,** and protections under the color of law, you may very well be the next George Zimmerman. And frankly, even if you win, what type of life, property, or treasure will you have left?

There seems to be a pretty basic answer to this one: leave the policing of potential property crimes to the police. In this way you have a clear cut argument that you were defending against injury and/or death. As I teach my young officers, be your own risk manager! Just because you can legally do something, is it really necessary, and are you willing to face the political fallout?

There is no bright line standard for us to refer to in order to guarantee a successful outcome if we are forced to utilize a high level of force to defend. My experience shows that there is a significant political aspect to how these cases are prosecuted which I will address in chapter five. It is imperative that you understand how the system works if you become entangled in our court system. It may be considered the best in the world, but it is far from perfect.

The Court System:

There are many ways you can be criminally or civilly charged after a defensive use of force incident. Our system of law has two separate court systems, federal and state. We will discuss the state court system first.

State Court:

For you, the defendant, to be criminally charged, there must be probable cause that a crime has been committed by you. Criminal cases are normally investigated by law enforcement and then the decision to prosecute is made by a prosecuting attorney who works for the state and locality. The prosecuting attorney can bring your case to court by obtaining a warrant for your arrest based on probable cause or he can choose to have you indicted with the use of a grand jury. Either way you end up in court and must defend yourself.

If there is no probable cause for a warrant or indictment you can still find yourself in state court based on a civil court case where probable cause of a crime is not required. The best way to explain civil law is that it is intended to make the aggrieved party (plaintiff) whole with some type of civil penalty such as money. In reality anyone can sue anyone for any reason if they wish to take the time to do so.

Federal Court:

If your use of force in self-defense does not end up in your states court system, you relax and breathe a sigh of relief and go on with your chaotic life. Not so fast; now the federal government gets a crack at you. Federal civil rights violations and criminal violations are investigated by the Justice Department in the form of the Federal Bureau of Investigation (FBI). And yes the system is quite similar to the state system where a U.S. Attorney can charge you based on probable cause, or the U.S. Attorney can empanel a grand jury to determine probable cause.

It is true that you cannot be charged with the same crime in both state court and federal court, but concurrent investigations can, and are, conducted with the sharing of information. If there are inappropriate or weak charges at the state level, the federal level can and will move forward. And the opposite is also true.

Self Defense Keys:
How do we prove that a use of force in self-defense was actually self-defense? There are some simple concepts that can be referred to:

- The defensive actions must be required in order to extract oneself from the situation. Once the situation changes where you are not in fear of death or serious bodily injury you no longer have the legal right to utilize a high level of physical force.
- An individual must be protecting themselves, family, or another from imminent harm of serious physical injury, and/or death. The force used in defense must be responding to an imminent threat.
- The defensive actions and subsequent force being used must be objectively reasonable under the circumstances.

Objectively Reasonable:
- Objectively reasonable is clearly the legal standard for use of self-defense physical techniques or weapon(s).
- Objectively reasonable is in the eye of the individual under assault or judged by a reasonable person in similar circumstances.
- Objectively reasonable must take into consideration the many confrontational factors that are applicable to the event such as age, size, sex, abilities, fitness level, and any other applicable considerations.
- Objectively reasonable has no clear bright line standard. In other words your self-defense will be judged by its own merits, there are no clear rules of engagement.

The Law as Applicable to Firearms:

If you choose to own and carry a firearm for self-defense you must know the law in your State, County, City, or Town! Find out the answers to all these questions prior to owning a firearm that you may have to use to defend yourself and/or your family!!!

- Is it legal to own a firearm in your home?
  Yes the Supreme Court of The United States (SCOTUS) "Heller" decision decided this
- Is it legal to carry a firearm outside your home?
  Varies from state to state
- Is it legal to transport a firearm in your vehicle?

Varies from state to state
- Is it legal to open carry a firearm?
  Varies from state to state
- Is it legal to conceal carry a firearm?
  Varies from state to state

Stand Your Ground Laws:

The most well know self-defense law seems to be the "stand your ground" laws that have been enacted in 30 or more states. Although each of these states has a somewhat different version of a stand your ground law the basic premise is pretty much the same.

The stand your ground premise is precisely what it sounds like. The individual who is exercising their ultimate human right of self-defense has no duty to retreat if they reasonably believe that using lethal force is necessary to prevent death or serious bodily harm to themselves or another.

I would be remiss not to point out that there is nothing wrong with a tactical retreat to allow the attacker the option to flee. The basics of this very important type of law are to not put the burden of retreating on the person being violently attacked. The first and primary concern must be the protection of family and self. If you focus, or are overly concerned with the intellectual analysis of the totality of the circumstances during this highly stressful and dangerous encounter where it is clear to all with any amount of commonsense that hesitation could be, and has been in past encounters, fatal, you have sealed your fate.

"Commonsense is decidedly uncommon"
—**Unknown**

Federal Law:

Federalist # 46 (James Madison):
The influence of the state and federal governments are compared in this essay. Madison's view of the relationship between state and federal governments, are discussed where Madison argued that the power behind the governments actually lay with the people. Madison felt this power was because Americans, through state militias, were armed. "Let a regular army, fully equal to the resources of the country, be formed; and let it be entirely at the devotion of the federal government; still it would not be going too far to say, that the State governments, with the people on their side, would be able to repel the danger".[15]

Second Amendment:
"A well-regulated Militia, being necessary to the security of a free State, the right of the people to keep and bear Arms, shall not be infringed".

Supreme Court of the United States Landmark Case (SCOTUS): (District of Columbia v. Heller)
Dick Heller was a special police officer in the District of Columbia. The District refused Heller's application to register

---

15   Madison, James. Federalist # 46.

a handgun he wished to keep in his home. Heller filed this lawsuit in the Federal District Court for the District of Columbia on Second Amendment grounds. Heller sought an injunction against enforcement of the bar on handgun registration, the licensing requirement prohibiting the carrying of a firearm in the home without a license, and the trigger-lock requirement insofar as it prohibits the use of functional firearms within the home.

The Heller case, decided by a 5-to-4 vote, struck down a ban on handguns kept in the home for self-defense, saying it violated the Second Amendment (SCOTUS)

Decision:

The handgun ban and the trigger-lock requirement (as applied to self-defense) violate the Second Amendment. The total ban on handgun possession in the home amounts to a prohibition on an entire class of arms that Americans overwhelmingly choose for the lawful purpose of self-defense. This prohibition would fail constitutional muster under any standard of scrutiny. Similarly, the requirement that any lawful firearm in the home be disassembled or bound by a trigger lock makes it impossible for citizens to use arms for the core lawful purpose of self-defense and is therefore unconstitutional.

The Court ruled that a license for the firearm will satisfy Heller's prayer for relief and therefore does not address the constitutionality of the licensing requirement. Assuming Heller is not otherwise disqualified from exercising Second Amendment rights, the District of Columbia must permit him to register his handgun and must issue him a license to carry it in the home.

Issue:

The Second Amendment right is not a right to keep and carry any weapon in any manner and for any purpose. The Court has upheld gun control legislation including prohibitions on concealed weapons and possession of firearms by felons and the mentally ill, laws forbidding the carrying of firearms in sensitive places such as schools and government buildings, and laws imposing conditions and qualifications on the commercial sale of arms. The historical tradition of prohibiting the carrying of dangerous and unusual weapons supports the holding in United States v. Miller that the sorts of weapons protected are those in common use at the time.[16]

It is certainly worth noting that this decision was decided by a 5-4 vote and split by ideological philosophies. We will discuss this further in chapter five, it is quite fascinating to delve into the political leanings of federal judges.

A Fair Minded Non-Political Stance:

- This author supports the Supreme Court of the United States (SCOTUS) "Heller" decision that the people have the right to own and keep a firearm in their homes for self-defense in **all** 50 States.
- This author supports the ultimate human right of self-defense and defense of others.
- This author believes in the ultimate human obligation of self-defense and defense of others.

---

16   District of Columbia v. Heller. SCOTUS 554 U.S.

- This author supports each individual states right to regulate the ownership, carrying, and use of firearms in keeping with the SCOTUS Heller decision, the Second Amendment, and the intent of the Bill of Rights and Constitution of the United States.
- This author strongly endorses the importance of training in the use of a firearm, or any other weapon, for self-defense.

In this next segment I will proceed with both statistical evidence and anecdotal evidence to defend my position on ownership of firearms for the sole purpose of self-defense. I make no claim that any of these statistics are accurate while conceding that statistics can and are used by experts on each side of this issue.

What I will defend and argue to the very end is for the absolute human right to self-defense and defense of others as a historically proven and morally accepted truth.

Statistical Evidence:

- According to Bureau of Justice Statistics numbers, each year between 1987 and 1992 about 62,200 victims of violent crimes used guns to defend themselves, while another 20,000 annually used guns to protect property.
- According to the National Self-Defense Survey conducted by criminology professor Gary Kleck of Florida State University in 1993, Americans used guns

2.3 million times a year to defend themselves between 1988 and 1993

- According to the Gun Owners Foundation (GOF), a non-profit, tax-deductible educational foundation, as many as 200,000 women use a gun every year to defend themselves against sexual abuse.
- According to the Clinton Justice Department, there are as many as 1.5 million cases of self-defense every year. The National Institute of Justice published this figure in 1997 as part of "Guns in America", a study which was authored by noted anti-gun criminologists Philip Cook and Jens Ludwig.
- Gary Kleck, Ph.D., a professor in the School of Criminology and Criminal Justice at Florida State University in Tallahassee, reports "handguns' are the weapon of choice for self-defense. Citizens use handguns to protect themselves over 1.9 million times a year".

Some of the statistics presented are very difficult to prove or disprove and are only used for the sake of argument. Regardless if these numbers are inflated there clearly are a large number of people using firearms for self-defense purposes.

Anecdotal Evidence:

Duluth, Ga. —An intruder who was shot and killed after a confrontation with a woman in her shower was likely stalking her for days and may have had other victims, police said. The 53-year-old woman, who is a school counselor, was alone. "The male was armed with a kitchen knife, (and) a struggle ensued between the two of them," a police spokesman said.

The woman tried to fight the man off with a shower rod, and he forced her into her bedroom. She grabbed a .22-caliber handgun and shot the man nine times. Police said the man ran out a back door and collapsed in the yard. He later died at a local medical center. Police said the shooting appeared to be justified, and that she acted in self-defense. There are no plans to charge her.

Houston, Texas —A teenage girl who was home alone says she was prepared to shoot when someone tried breaking into her family home. At approximately 3:30 p.m., the perpetrator tried cracking the code to her electronic front door lock. From the inside, the 17-year-old girl heard the alarm and went straight for her dad's Glock 19 handgun. She was trained by her dad to use it. Fortunately, the alarm scared the would-be intruder away.

As word spread about the home invasion attempt, neighbors say they're getting their guns ready too.

Glenville, Pa. —A man who kicked in the front door of a York County home found a woman waiting for him with her handgun at the ready, according to police. The 31-year-old woman was alone when she heard someone trying to force their way inside. She grabbed a handgun that she trains with on a regular basis, police said.

When the man eventually kicked in her front door and entered the home, the woman leveled the gun and told the intruder not to come any closer. He obeyed her order and was found on the front porch of a neighbor's home when an officer arrived minutes later. Police said he may have been intoxicated.

Understanding the Police Investigation:

Police are trained to develop probable cause to make an arrest. Many police officers have little or no experience in the investigation of self-defense homicides and are unclear of the rules of engagement. Police officers are like anyone else and have strong personal feelings in this arena. My experience has shown that the vast majority of law enforcement (L.E.) officers are pro self-defense for citizens when they use firearms or other weapons. This said, it does not mean that the management of the police organization is as pro self-defense as the investigator may be.

L.E. will secure the entire crime scene which is your home in many self-defense cases. L.E. will collect evidence and seize whatever weapon you used to defend yourself or your family. L.E. will want to interview you, members of your family, and any other witness immediately.

You must be able to articulate your reason for your use of self-defense particularly when it involves a high level of force. To establish your justification you must include:

1. Primary aggressor- You must illustrate to the investigator that you did not wish to engage in mutual combat. Your only desire was for the attacker to leave you and your family unharmed. You used force because the attacker left you no reasonable alternative.

2. Imminent Fear- You must illustrate to the investigator that you were in imminent fear of serious injury or death to you, or family members. Even if the attacker was not armed it is possible to illustrate this concept based on the attacker's actions.

3. Confrontational Factors- You must illustrate to the investigator that the attacker had superior options such as size, youth, numbers, weapons, or any other reasonable advantages. The fact that you felt the need to safeguard you family puts you at a disadvantage as well and should be explained.

4. Duty to Retreat v. Stand Your Ground- Some states require citizens to retreat if safe to do so, or at least leave the attacker an escape route. Many other states have stand your ground laws which does not require either. Even if you are sure of your state's laws and choose to stand your ground it never hurts to be able to make an argument to the investigator that that you verbally ordered the attacker to leave you alone.

5. The Home (Castle Doctrine)- All states view you defending your home in a more liberal light. At least 46 states have a castle doctrine where there are more specific guidelines on deadly force. In most, the duty to retreat is not required but it becomes clearer to the investigator if you can make an argument that you either took a position of cover to allow the intruder to leave or that you were forced to confront the intruder because of family members in the home about whom you were highly concerned.

L.E. needs to be led in the right direction. Having an understanding of what is required to show justification for the self-defense can allow the investigator to close the investigation with little disruption to your life or that of your family. Although some will argue that you should always have a lawyer with you and a prepared statement I do not necessarily agree.

This can look very suspicious to L.E. and can be construed as confrontational. If you are comfortable with the law and calm enough, give a brief statement to the investigator in a clear and concise manner. Do not ramble or get too detailed. Just provide the basics to establish justification for self-defense. If you are uncomfortable, or questions get excessively confrontational or disturbing, do not hesitate at any time to ask for an attorney.

Brevity with few details is critical. There is much evidence that shows people do not remember details well in any stressful situation. It is very likely that your memory will not be completely accurate with specific details of the confrontation, and that your account of the event will differ with other witnesses. This is quite normal!

Memory Lapses:

The "Hopkins Study" found that:

- When people devoted themselves to visual tasks they experienced auditory exclusion.
- When people devoted themselves to auditory tasks they experienced visual exclusion.

- "When attention is deployed to one modality, it necessarily extracts a cost on another modality. The brain can't simultaneously give full attention to both".
  Dr. Steven Yantis, Department of Psychological and Brain Sciences. Johns Hopkins University.[17]

Dr. Honig & Dr. Roland researched 348 police involved shootings and found:

- The officer had no recollection of the gun discharging
- Officers gave conflicting statements
- There were significant time distortions
- Audio exclusion occurred based on tunnel vision
- Officers experienced temporary paralysis
- Officers had significant memory distortion
- It is interesting to note that this study showed that perceptual distortion also occurred in witnesses not just those involved in the high stress encounter.
  —Dr. Honig & Dr. Roland[18]

Based on the complexities of any legal system, including ours in the United States, it should be quite clear to the reader how normal confusion and discrepancies in statements can become quite an issue in court proceedings. It would be nice to believe that police investigators, prosecuting attorneys,

---

17 Yantis, Steven. Hopkins Study. Force Science News. August 1, 2005.
18 Honig, A.L. & Roland, J.E. Shots Fired Officer Involved. The Police Chief. October 1998.

and judges have a solid understanding of these issues but my experience has shown that they do not.

Self-defense training, in particular that of firearms, must include some basic discussion of our system of law, some historical context, and federal, state, and local laws. It will be amazing to the reader to see the difference in laws relating to firearms from state to state.

It is also critical for the reader to understand the importance of hiring an experienced attorney who is expert in the field of self-defense and shaping public opinion prior to being charged with a criminal offense, either state or federal. I would recommend consulting with an attorney regardless of how you believe the investigation is going if at any time you believe that charges may be forthcoming. Even if you decided to provide a statement early on without an attorney you should at least have one on call for follow up questioning.

The **original statement is your story**. With **questioning, the story becomes that of the investigating officer.** This may seem like an overly paranoid stance, but rest assured I have seen cases prosecuted solely for political reasons.

Never understate the importance of a seasoned informed attorney. Getting out in front of a highly charged and potentially political issue is critical. Shaping public opinion is also critical. I know that I would not hesitate to engage an attorney if the need arises!

What in the world does shaping public opinion mean? In the political world, everything! A competent attorney can utilize the press as a tool to get the appropriate message of self-defense out to the public. In today's world of social media, blogs, tweets, and all the other electronic methods of communicating, the message is in public view immediately. In most cases whomever gets the message out first wins the public opinion war regardless of truth and accuracy.

Judges, juries, and elected officials make decisions based on public opinion more often than not. It takes a very strong individual to ignore what friends and neighbors think and expect!

CHAPTER FOUR

THE MECHANICAL ADVANTAGE

If you are still reading I will assume that you are a convert to the concept of the ultimate human right. My intent with this chapter is to discuss the philosophy of self-defense. There are many programs, and books, that discuss the nuts and bolts of how to defend yourself. Many of these resources are outstanding and I do not feel the need to compete, but rather to explain what many of these training forums leave out. Martial arts programs at your local dojo, community programs with local police, firearms training classes, expert discussions and presentations all have merit.

Philosophy v. Training:

This chapter is not intended to provide self-defense training; it is intended to be educational only. There is a significant difference between training and education. Training is the "how to" method of instruction. It is the hands on part of self-defense and is a must do for successful learning. Education is the philosophical and cerebral portion of learning. I hope that the following information will assist the reader in evaluating any training programs that they may wish to attend, or to be a better educated, better prepared, less vulnerable target.

To help the reader understand where I am coming from I intend to discuss some basic principles of how we learn, retain, and act under stress. All self-defense concepts must take these basic principles into consideration for realistic application during difficult and stressful encounters. If your program does not consider these three basic tenets you may be getting some solid cardio exercise but you are not receiving self-defense training.

The three basic tenets of self-defense are the understanding that:

1. "Actions are always faster than reactions", and "the human brain reverts to automatic responses".
2. "To teach a person nothing, teach them everything".
3. "Mindset and resolve must be present, if not you have already lost".

**Actions Are Always Faster Than Reactions/
Automatic Responses:**

How do we know this? Well other than a huge amount of anecdotal evidence, there is science to back this up. The Human Brain works in two primary ways.

1. The Cortex (Upper Brain):
   a. Logic
   b. Rational thinking
   c. Slow actions allowing decision making and problem solving
   d. Excludes threats requiring immediate response
2. The Limbic System (Mid Brain):
   a. Automatic responses relating to high levels of arousal
   b. Dominates the upper brain and reduces ability to think rationally and problem solve with logic
   c. Is action oriented

When levels of arousal (stress) are increased the mid-brain takes over. The best that can be expected is for prior training (preparation) to become your automatic response. To better illustrate this concept and the relationship between arousal and performance studies by Researchers Robert M. Yerkes and John D. Dodson are quite helpful.

Robert M. Yerkes and John D. Dodson:
Arousal is a major aspect of many learning theories and is closely related to other concepts, such as anxiety, attention, agitation,

stress, and motivation. The arousal level can be thought of as how much capacity you have available to work with. One finding, as reported by Robert M. Yerkes and John D. Dodson predicts an inverted U-shaped function between arousal and performance. A certain amount of arousal can increase your ability to perform; too much or too little arousal decreases your ability to perform. You want some mid-level of arousal to provide maximum performance.

Too little arousal has an inert effect on the person, while too much has a hyperactive effect. For example, very low levels of arousal in an athletic event results in poor performance. You have little or no adrenaline flowing, hence the pre-game warmup, which prepares the athlete to perform from the beginning of the event. In contrast very high levels of arousal can cause stress in the athlete where they "choke" whether kicking a field goal or shooting a free throw.

To relate this to self-defense exceptionally high levels of arousal (stress) can cause total panic and/or the body to shut down all automatic responses. In simple terms the person being attacked will freeze up and hesitate, or take no action at all. No one is exempt from this "human condition". Regardless of how well trained you are this can and does happen.

In the self-defense arena arousal is basically being alert, physically and mentally. Various body systems and hormones are involved, and contribute to alertness and readiness to move.

Performance is the ability to defend yourself and others against an attacker. Performance begins with advance preparation to defend, which centers around a mindset of tough mindedness and resolve. The goal clearly is to hurt your attacker before he can hurt you.[19]

To Teach Nothing, Teach Everything

How do we know this? Again other than a huge amount of anecdotal evidence, we also have science to back this up.

Hick's Law (W. E. Hicks, Quarterly Journal of Experimental Psychology, 1952):

Hick's Law states that the time required to make a decision is a function of the number of available options. It is used to estimate how long it will take for people to make a decision when presented with multiple choices. For example, when a person must decide from a number of different self-defense options, Hick's Law predicts that the greater the number of alternative self-defense options, the longer it will take to make the decision and select the correct one.[20]

Hick's Law has implications for the design of any self-defense system that requires too many complex alternatives. In reality, if your self-defense training of choice is so complex that you must go back again and again to "recall" the techniques and concepts it is time to find a new program.

Even if your life is that of self-defense and/or fight sports competition and you are highly trained, you more than likely have only a few techniques that you fall back on during times of stress when competing. This is like having a favorite move

19   Yerkes, Robert M & Dodson, John D. The Relation of Stress of Stimulus to Rapidity of Habit Formation. October 2004.
20   Hicks, William Edmund. Hicks Law, Wikipedia.

when you play basketball, or a go to shot when you play tennis. When the chips are down the smart competitor reverts to his best option.

So...the reader now is aware of how critical the KISS principle (keep it simple stupid) is, which should assist us in the choices of how we prepare to defend.

Mindset and Resolve Must Be Present, or You Have Already Lost:

How do I know this?
I have reviewed literally thousands of police use of force cases and the number one factor where an officer gets hurt is when the officer hesitates to use force and/or uses too little force. It is quite clear that hesitation, and lack of preparation kills.

I know from personal experience how it feels to be attacked when the attacker has the desire to hurt and/or kill you. I have been attacked with edged weapons, firearms, fists/feet/teeth, and whatever was handy. I survived early in my career out of sheer luck as I was clearly unprepared and hesitated on many occasions. I survived later in my career because I no longer held back or hesitated to use force in my defense of self or in the defense of others.

I have served as an expert witness in state and federal courts for police use of force and civilian self-defense numerous times and have found that in both arenas human beings are reluctant to utilize force, especially an extreme level of force.

"Out of every hundred men, ten shouldn't even be there, eighty are just targets, nine are the real fighters, and we are lucky to have them. Ah, but the one, one is a warrior, and he will bring the others back".
—**Heraclitus** 500 BC

You must be willing to hurt another human being or you are better off not physically resisting at all! Strikes and techniques that do not have any chance to incapacitate an attacker, do nothing more than enrage and motivate an attacker. Poor training with unrealistic techniques and tactics are a recipe for disaster.

"I am thankful to those who said "no", because of them I did it myself".
—**Albert Einstein**

The Mechanical Advantage:

You have two basic choices of modes of self-defense, empty hand or armed. One does not preclude the other. If you feel confident in your ability to defend without a weapon, it is helpful to understand that your assailant may be armed, or there may be multiple assailants which puts you at a distinct disadvantage. If you choose to go the armed defense route you still will need to do some basic preparation for empty hand defense. This is for several reasons; you may not always have your weapon of choice, your weapon of choice may fail, or someone may wish to take your weapon of choice away.

This chapter will advocate for armed defense for a number of reasons. I refer to the old adage of engineers; "Obtain a mechanical advantage whenever possible". This simply means, why use hand strength if you have a wrench, why use body weight if you have a lever? Tools are our friends.

A weapon is simply a tool to assist us in performing a task that may otherwise be too dangerous, to difficult, or impossible to accomplish.

"Do what you can with what you have, where you are".
—Theodore Roosevelt

Empty hand:
The significant advantage with personal weapons such as hands, elbows, knees, and feet is that you are never caught short. Your weapons are always with you. The other advantage is that even when you have a mechanical advantage (weapon) you may have to revert to personal weapons if the weapon fails or is lost.

The disadvantages are obvious. You must be up close and personal to utilize personal weapons, and you must be well trained and prepared. Your physical attributes are also part of the equation, even if many will argue this point. Bigger, stronger, and faster is always an advantage. They are not the only factors in a confrontation but they are important ones.

Weapons Discussion:
What is a weapon? There are many. In reality most anything can be used as a weapon. I will focus on the type weapons that

seem most prevalent in our society and discuss the positives and negatives of each type weapon. There is a clear choice to this author and I will discuss said choice last.

Weapon of Opportunity (blunt object, keys, sharp object):
The advantage is just what you are thinking; I have this object with me. The disadvantages are numerous. You probably have not trained in the use of the weapon of opportunity, you are up close and personal with these type weapons, and most disconcerting is the fact that any weapon can be taken from you and used against you.

Chemical Weapons (Pepper spray (OC),
blended sprays (OC, CS):
Utilizing a pepper type spray (Oleoresin capsicum) can give you a significant advantage. It slows and inhibits the attacker but does not stop the attacker in their tracks as the manufacture would have you believe. You can deploy this weapon from a distance and it is a less than lethal choice (non-deadly force). If you consider this type weapon as a method to gain an advantage it may be a solid choice.

The self-defense spray normally will cause the eyes to shut, and breathing to be restricted. It is very uncomfortable to the person exposed but it is not going to stop a motivated attacker.

The disadvantages are also significant. You need to have access to the spray; it can't be buried in your pocket, book bag, or purse. It is difficult to hit your attacker in the face during a confrontation. If you use the spray it will be fairly up close to the attacker and you will be contaminated as well. Even if you use the spray from a distance if your attacker grapples with you, you will be contaminated. The spray can be taken away from you and used against you.

There can also be a significant false sense of security if you incorrectly believe that the chemical will always be effective and you do not need any other preparation. I have been exposed to OC and CS chemicals a number of times and though unpleasant it is not incapacitating.

Electronic Devices (Conductive Energy Devices (CED)):

The stun gun is a great tool and works the vast majority of the time if you have immediate access to the weapon (not buried in your pocket, book bag, or purse), if you hit your target and both darts enter (pierce) the skin so you have a completed circuit, and if the weapon is charged and operating correctly. You can deploy this weapon from a distance and it is a less than lethal choice (non-deadly force). Again, I have been exposed to a stun weapon and it is highly effective when deployed correctly, but it can and does fail.

The CED, if not maintained properly, may not work. It needs a proper charge to be deployed. If you miss your intended target your only other option is to use the CED as a contact weapon in the "drive stun mode" where you must be up close and personal.

Edged Weapons:

A knife is a very ugly weapon that most people are unable to deploy. It is up close and personal and difficult to hold on to in a bloody violent confrontation. It can be taken from you and used against you. The knife is very lethal (deadly force), in many cases as lethal, or more lethal than a firearm. I do not know many folks who have the resolve to stab someone with a knife, but it's a great method of defense if it is your weapon of choice, and if you are well trained in its use.

I hesitate to recommend a knife but would not be opposed to one based on the individuals knowledge, skill, and physical ability to utilize one.

Firearms:

A firearm is the weapon of choice for many. Its clear advantage is that it is the most lethal and simplistic to use. Its clear disadvantage is that it is the most lethal and simplistic to use. This seems counter intuitive to have the same statement as both positive and negative, but such is not the case.

The facts are that the lethality of a firearm is a positive for the person employing the firearm to stop most threats. The fact that it is simplistic to use allows almost anyone to use the firearm as a self-defense option.

In contrast, the fact that a firearm is so lethal makes it an unforgiving choice if used against a person who is not a deadly threat or a family member who you did not challenge and/or recognize. Because a firearm is so simplistic, many folks refuse to accept the fact that training in the use of a firearm is critical.

I would imagine that the reader is nodding their head and saying "yup, very very true".

Firearms Training Keys & Why Self-Defense
Is So Different From Target Shooting:

Self-defense shooting is completely unlike target shooting. Though it is quite clear to the experts I have spoken to that for self-defense shooting to be effective the person defending with a firearm must have been taught the basics of marksmanship, and must accept that in the stress of an attack, marksmanship principles are only utilized if these principles have been practiced and ingrained as an automatic response (Mid-brain).

The reader would be amazed by how many police shootings occur at very close range and how many times both the assailant and the police officers miss their intended target. In fact, some of the more positive reports I have read state that L.E. only hit their intended target 33% of the time.

When involved in a frightening life threatening confrontation, studies have shown time and time again that human beings will experience a number of physical and emotional realities. Phenomenon such as tunnel vision, auditory exclusion, the loss of fine and complex motor control, irrational behavior, and the inability to think clearly have all been observed as part of a deadly encounter.

Principles of self-defense shooting are based on science which shows us that in a stressful encounter the human brain will be utilizing the "limbic", or "mid-brain" portion. This simply means that your body will revert to gross motor skills and "tunnel vision" will occur. You will respond with whatever training you have received, if you are fortunate and do not completely panic. If you are properly trained these basic principles will become part of your mid-brain response.

This human condition is based on science such as the "Yerkes-Dodson Law Inverted U". The Inverted "U" shows us that as your levels of arousal (stress) increase, your level of performance becomes more acute, and then deteriorates rapidly. Studies have shown that you should expect:

- Your fine motor skills to deteriorate
- Your family to be confused
- Your family to do what you trained them to. If there is no plan you can only hope that you and your family guess correctly

"Prior planning prevents poor performance".
—Unknown

As described in the "Yerkes Dodson Inverted U" discussed previously, there is no earthly way any of us will react rationally and cognitively apply basic marksmanship principles during a highly stressful encounter. Science has shown us that the best chance you have to perform is to draw from training that has proven to be simple, realistic, and stress tested.

This may seem arbitrary but your ability to perform in highly stressful situations may have nothing to do with a self-defense type situation where you perform well under stress. It may simply be in your background that you regularly deal with stress such as construction work in high places where you must focus completely as to not fall and injure or kill yourself. But even if you naturally perform well under stress, training in the basics is critical to your success.

For the rest of us, who may not have this type of background, it is imperative to seek and take part in training that can be drawn from, if needed. This training must involve some type of simulation scenario based decision making exercises that induce stress in the attendee. As previously stated, this book is not the "how to" that many others have written, in fact there are numerous experts in the field of firearms, deadly encounters, and self-defense. They are very worthwhile readings, and for those with an interest, seek them out!

I continue to attempt to make this clear because I have been very offended many times when I have read short essays or seen a short video that makes the claim to prepare you to defend yourself without ever getting up from your armchair. This is an educational essay. For the reader to prepare to exercise their absolute human right and absolute human obligation the reader must spend some time learning and preparing with physical activity and skills training.

I now will spend some time discussing the pitfalls of a home defense firearm and some preparation that should be done if you choose to own one. The reader hopefully is educated and informed enough to accept that simply purchasing a firearm and storing the firearm somewhere in the home is not a realistic plan for success.

Firearms Basics and Safety:
If you have decided to, or already have purchased a firearm, the most important education you can receive is how to be **safe**. Any time you handle or shoot your firearm safety is of

paramount concern. As a responsible firearms owner you should be governed by the following safety rules!

1. **Cardinal Rules of Firearms Safety:**
   - Never point a firearm (loaded or unloaded) at anyone you are not justified in shooting.
   - Treat every firearm as if it were loaded.

2. **General Rules of Firearms Safety:**
   - Do not let your family and friends make a conversation piece of your home defense firearm.
   - Do not let family or friends handle your home defense firearm unsupervised.
   - Do not leave firearms and ammunition where they are accessible to children. The child, who has not seen or feels the damage a real firearm can cause, finds it hard to believe "Daddy's / Mommy's Gun" is dangerous. The desire to "show off" may prompt a child to obtain a weapon and let others play with it.
   - Keep a record of the make, model, and serial number of your firearm in a safe location. Report the theft of your firearm to local L.E. immediately. The more people who know you own a firearm for home defense the more vulnerable you are to theft of said firearm.
   - Do not dry fire or practice with your weapon when small children or irresponsible persons are present. This prompts them to play with the weapon. When dry firing inside the home use an outside wall of

masonry construction for practice. If an accident should occur, the round will not travel throughout the home or through several apartments.

- Common experience demands that all firearms should be kept out of reach of children and immature or irresponsible adults.

- Weapons and ammunition should be locked out of sight whenever you are away from home. A responsible firearm owners concern should extend itself to any neighborhood children or adults who might visit the home.

Storage of Firearm in the Home:

It is critical that the home defense firearm is kept in a secure place. I recognize that the question of easy access v. security is always a difficult one. When determining your personal plan for storage of your firearm please keep the following in mind:

- Your primary reason for securing your firearm is to prevent injury and unauthorized access. Please remember that easy access for you in many cases is easy access for a family member. In the wrong persons hands a firearm is the ultimate final tragedy.

- Minimize theft opportunity. It continues to amaze me how many home defense weapons are stolen each year and utilized in crimes. This can be embarrassing, and distressing if someone is hurt, when the police come to advise you that your firearm has been used in a crime. There may also be some potential liability if you did not exercise reasonable caution to prevent the theft if it ends up being a family member or friend who has stolen the firearm.

Access v. Security in Firearm Ownership:

Safety is paramount, but access to be able to defend is also critical. Develop a plan of action as to where your home defense weapon is stored and what steps must be taken to arm said weapon to be able to defend.

The plan you develop must be simple and easy to remember. Plans that involve too many details and seem "all consuming" may overwhelm your family and create undue stress and fear.

Only you know how much information is appropriate for your children, keeping in mind self-defense is the primary responsibility of the adult. Every person and family is different. A plan that works for one family may be unworkable for another. If you keep these safety rules in mind, you and your family should be able to develop a safe plan of action for personal home defense.

Questions such as: where do you store you firearm, and should the firearm be loaded or unloaded must be addressed.

Loaded v. Unloaded:

- Time is critical; can you access and load your home defense weapon in time?
- Have you trained (practiced)?
- Does your family have access?
- What is the age of family, firearms experience of family, maturity of family?

- Other pertinent factors?
- Are you more concerned for intruders or accidental discharge of weapons by children?

Some Basic Recommendations:

I advocate for a "Three step rule of access". Prior to you being able to discharge your home firearm the home defender should need to make three separate actions (movements)

Example:

1. Wake up and exit bed.
2. Retrieve firearm from safe but easily accessible location.
3. Seat cylinder **or** disengage safety.

This may seem time consuming, but it gives the home defender time to wake up and assess a threat if any. The potential of tragedy by discharging a firearm when partially asleep prior to assessing a threat can be devastating!

Engaging the threat:

When engaging a potential threat loud verbal commands such as "leave my home or I will shoot you" are critical.

Why are verbal's so important:

Is there a legal requirement to warn an intruder prior to defending yourself and your family? Would a verbal warning give the intruder an advantage? There does not seem to be a "bright line" rule on this, though I advocate for a verbal warning for a variety of reasons:

- A verbal warning can prevent shooting the wrong person. When you shout out it gives the suspected intruder time to identify himself.
- A verbal warning will always will be favorably looked on, if litigation occurs, if you are forced to utilize deadly force against an intruder.
- A verbal warning gives the intruder the opportunity to flee your home.
- A verbal warning gives your family advance warning to take cover.
- A verbal warning forces you to breath prior to shooting.

It is also so important to discuss what firearms experts call the "Universal Cover Mode". The vast majority of the time anyone has a firearm in their hand the finger must be off the trigger! The only time the finger is on the trigger is if a deadly threat is identified and the shooter is justified in killing the person presenting the deadly threat.

The Universal Cover Mode:

There are continuing concerns of having accidental discharges with firearms. An unintentional discharge occurs when the home defender has his/her finger on the trigger of their weapon when the home defender has an involuntary contraction.

- Startle Effect: When a sudden unexpected occurrence frightens the home defender (i.e. loud noise)

- Postural Disturbance: When a sudden loss of balance causes the body to tighten/tense up (ex, losing one's footing)
- Interlimb Interaction: The muscles of one hand contract because the holder or subject suddenly moves, causing the other hand to contract

The Universal Cover Mode is recommended for the home defender to use to prevent unintentional discharges. The Universal Cover Mode is used along with verbalization skills "Leave my home the police are coming, or get on the ground or I will shoot". The subject must be directed by the home defender to react in such a manner that protects the home defender and allows for control of the situation.

The Cardinal Rule of the Universal Cover Mode: Keep your finger outside the trigger guard until you are on target and have **decided** to fire because of a deadly threat.

You should never attempt to place hands on a person with a weapon in one hand. Maintain a cover position until the police arrive. If you are assaulted, retreat, creating distance whenever possible. Distance is your friend when you have a firearm. Distance creates time to assess the threat and decide if deadly force is warranted. Distance does not provide the attacker an opportunity to grab you and attempt to take your firearm. If the attacker continues to close in on you, this sends a clear message to the person defending that they are a significant threat since they now are aware you are armed. A nonviolent person is unlikely to close the distance between an armed defender and himself.

In a review of confrontations with a firearm under stress, it has been proven that finger on the trigger is conducive to accidental discharges with catastrophic results. The **"Universal Cover Mode"** has been used by L.E. for many years and has been proven to be sound practice and a national standard for training.

Case Study (Mistaken Identity):

A soldier at Fort Bragg in Fayetteville, North Carolina, tried to bring his wife a surprise breakfast in bed Friday morning, but as his reward for the romantic gesture, he found himself in the hospital with a gunshot wound to the chest. Police believe the shooting was simply a mistake, but they continue to investigate the circumstances of the shooting.

Mr. Zia Segule left the home he shares with his wife Tiffany in Fayetteville. Tiffany stayed in bed, catching some extra sleep. But at about 10:15 a.m., Zia Segule unexpectedly came back home. He carried a take-out breakfast to surprise his sleeping wife. At least, he thought she was sleeping.

According to police, the soldier did not attempt to sneak into the house. He simply entered through the front door as he normally would. But in the interim between his departure and return, 27-year-old Tiffany had apparently activated the house's security alarm system. When Zia Segule walked through the door, the alarm went off.

The police say they still are not sure whether or not Zia attempted to tell his wife that he was home, or if he tried to shut off the alarm. All they say they know for sure is that Tiffany, perhaps nervous due to a series of break-ins in the area recently, pulled out a gun and fired one round sight unseen, through her closed bedroom door. The shot struck her husband in the chest.

Proper Steps for Preparing to Defend Your Home:

1. Obtain Home Defense Firearm:
   - This can be done while on phone with 911 operator but should be your first objective
   - Ensure your home defense firearm is loaded and ready to fire.
2. Calling 911:
   - This should be a preliminary step once your home defense weapon is located and made ready to fire. I recommend a second person handle the 911 call if possible.
   - Advise the 911 call taker that you are armed
   - Provide a description of the armed person, and the intruder if possible
   - Keep the 911 operator on the line
   - When L.E. arrives follow their commands; L.E. will still not know all the details of home owner v. intruder
3. Meet your family at a prearranged "safe location":
   - When the entire family is safe at a prearranged safe location loudly announce that you are armed and willing to utilize deadly force.
   - If your entire family is not at the prearranged location wait. Do not leave to search for missing family member except as a last resort.

- Have a "safe word" such as "mom" or "dad". This way everyone will know when it is safe to come out from hiding and if it is safe to enter the prearranged safe area.

4. How to Move as A family:
   - Moving as a family is done as a last resort to flee a home.
   - If your entire family is in prearranged safe area your best option is to stay armed and ready until L.E. arrives.
   - If you must flee the home, (fire, no or lengthy police response) do so as a group. The armed home defender should take the lead.
   - If the armed home defender knows where the intruder is, take a position of cover focusing on the known area of the intruder and order your family to exit home as a group. The armed person should exit the home last.

5. Clearing of Your Home:
   - You should not attempt to search or clear your home if entire family is safe and waiting for police response.
   - If a family member is missing you must weigh your options. You may be leaving other family members defenseless while searching.
   - If this is your decision, then move quickly but carefully thru the home. As you are moving utilize light by turning on lights prior to entering rooms.

- As you are moving, firmly announce that you are armed and will shoot if threatened.
- Utilize safe words when moving in areas you think your missing family member is located.
- Remember it is much safer to stay in a prearranged location forcing the intruder to find you.

6. Multiple firearms in home defense situation:
   - I recommend against this. There have been numerous cases of "friendly fire" with L.E. and Military who are well trained. Although I would change this recommendation based on the level of training and experience of the firearms owners.

7. Interacting with L.E. when they arrive:
   - You should still be on the phone with 911.
   - 911 will let you know when L.E. has arrived.
   - You have advised them that you are armed.
   - Do not rush to meet L.E. Tell the 911 operator where you are located and what you are wearing. Comply if L.E. asks you to exit your home and meet them if you believe it is safe to do so.
   - L.E. normally will announce their presence as they enter your home. Respond to them and tell them you are the homeowner and that you have secured your firearm.
   - L.E. will normally order you to put your firearm down. Comply with all their commands for your safety and theirs.

- L.E. will normally order you to show them your hands. Comply and do not make sudden movements.
- L.E. will normally ask you for I.D. to prove that you are the homeowner or that you belong there.
- L.E. will normally respond with several officers and some may continue searching for the intruder while a primary officer interacts with you.
- Be prepared to answer questions quickly. L.E. will want as much information as possible to ensure that they can clear your home and begin searching for the intruder(s).

Prearranged Safe Location:

- Try to stay away from a personal bedroom where the home defender may be surprised by frightened family member and not have time to assess the threat.
- Should have access to outside through window or porch for escape is needed.
- Should have enough space and clear view of doorway.
- Should not have multiple entrances/exits. It is difficult to cover multiple areas of access.

Safe Word:
Should be

- Simple to remember
- Personal to your family

- Have no similarity to words like "help", "No", or other terms used when aid is needed.

These guidelines are suggestions only and may be altered or modified based on needs of family and skill level of the home defender. I do not presume to have all the answers to such a complex issue of firearms defense.

I have a number of good friends with significant firearms background who disagree with me, particularly as it pertains to the "three step rule". To head off any of my detractors, and there are some, perhaps a two-step rule better fits your defense plan. What I am trying to avoid with firearms is the tragedy that can so easily occur without basic safeguards in place.

I would imagine that this chapter raised as many questions as it has answered! If this is the case I am content. I would far rather you discuss these issues with your family or a well-respected expert and tailor your plan to meet your needs and those of you and your family's lifestyle prior to any event occurring. Even if you take few or none of my suggestions, hopefully this chapter will engage you in thought and preparation. If a conversation takes place between you and your family I feel that I have been hugely successful!

CHAPTER FIVE

THE POLITICS OF FIREARMS

The reader may ask why the politics of firearms has any bearing on an individual's exercising of the ultimate human right and the ultimate human obligation. Sadly, it can have a significant impact on any citizen who is forced to defend and utilizes a high level of force. This is by far my favorite chapter to write and I believe the most relevant and eye opening information for the reader.

SCOTUS's Recent Decision on
District of Columbia v. Heller:
As discussed in chapter three, I mentioned the political ramifications in reference to the "Heller" case. The case, decided

by a 5-to-4 vote, struck down a ban on handguns kept in the home for self-defense, saying it violated the 2nd Amendment.

The first glaring issue to the reader quite obviously is the five to four decision! The SCOTUS 5-4 ruling struck down the District of Columbia's ban on handguns. Other major cities such as Chicago, San Francisco, New York have been forced to reconsider their respective ordinances.

This decision clearly reflects the incredible philosophical differences between conservatives and liberals on the U.S. Supreme Court.

The majority opinion was upheld by Justice Scalia, Chief Justice John Roberts, Justice Samuel Alito, Justice Anthony Kennedy, and Justice Clarence Thomas.

Providing the dissenting opinion were Justice John Paul Stevens, Justice Stephen Breyer, Justice Ruth Bader Ginsburg, and Justice David Souter.

Clearly the decision was made based on not only party line and philosophical differences, but it also reflects significant philosophical differences in how cities, overwhelmed with gun violence, and rural areas view gun ownership. The SCOTUS had not conclusively interpreted the 2nd Amendment since its ratification in 1791 until this case.

It does not take a constitutional scholar to understand why nine brilliant judicial minds were unable to agree with what appears on the surface such a simple interpretation of the 2nd Amendment. At first blush it would seem that this decision should have been 9-0 to strike down such a restrictive ordinance that clearly violates the intent of the 2nd Amendment.

This case did not attempt to address the extent to which the right to have a gun for protection in the home may extend outside the home, or long-standing prohibitions on the possession of firearms by felons or the mentally ill, or laws forbidding the carrying of firearms in sensitive places such as schools and government buildings, or concealed and open carry laws, or rifles, or extended magazines, or any other complex issue.

An argument could have been made for the dissenting votes if any of these hot button topics had been part of this case, but they were not! This case addressed the very simple question; can a citizen of the United States have a firearm *accessible* in their home for self-defense to exercise the "ultimate human right"?

Statements by politicians:

- Former Democratic presidential candidate and current president, Barack Obama, stated "the court did not find an unfettered right to bear arms" and that the ruling "will provide much-needed guidance to local jurisdictions across the country."

- Former Democratic Mayor Richard Daley called the ruling "very frightening" and stated "there will be more violence and higher taxes to pay for extra police if his city's gun restrictions are lost".

- Former Republican presidential candidate John McCain stated "This ruling is a landmark victory for 2nd Amendment freedom."

- Former President George Bush stated "I applaud the Supreme Court's historic decision today confirming what has always been clear in the Constitution: the 2nd Amendment protects an individual right to keep and bear firearms."

- Justice Scalia states the Constitution does not permit "the absolute prohibition of handguns held and used for self-defense in the home." Justice Scalia also stated that "the handgun is Americans' preferred weapon of self-defense in part because it can be pointed at a burglar with one hand while the other hand dials the police."

- Former D.C. Mayor Adrian Fenty commented "More handguns in the District of Columbia will only lead to more handgun violence".

- Wayne LaPierre (NRA) states "I consider this the opening salvo in a step-by-step process of providing relief for law-abiding Americans everywhere that have been deprived of this freedom".

- Plaintiff Dick Heller advised "I'm thrilled I am now able to defend myself and my household in my home".

The Political Climate:

The reader should begin to see how basic politics will not only affect a citizen's right to own and bear arms, but how a citizen will be treated if they are forced to use a firearm in self-defense. Federal judges, to include SCOTUS justices, are appointed by the sitting president for life terms.

The SCOTUS's primary focus and reason for existing is to rule on issues of constitutionality. On a reflective note, if there had been one more liberal justice as opposed to a conservative the decision would have been to uphold the D.C. ordinance. This would have led to many people being unable to defend themselves, with a mechanical advantage, and their family in their own home.

Where you live also has a significant impact on your right to self-defense. What region of the country do you live in? Do you live in an urban city, or a rural county? It can even come down to what congressional district you live in.

The Northeast generally has restrictive firearms laws; the Southeast normally has less restrictive firearms laws. The West coast seems to be more restrictive while the Midwest is all over the map so to speak. The best predictor of firearms laws seems to be the difference between urban and rural areas.

Pew Research Center: Social and Demographic Trends Project (July 15, 1014): [21]

Demographics of Gun Ownership:

Region
West	34%
Midwest	35%
South	38%
Northeast	27%

Environment:
Urban	22%
Suburban	36%
Rural	51%

---

21   Pew Research Center. Social and Demographic Trends Project. July 15, 2014.

Party Affiliation:
Republican   49%
Democrat   22%
Independent   37%

Yes, politics comes into everything as it pertains to exercising your ultimate human right. When you look towards L.E. to take a position on firearms laws, look no further than the difference between a police chief and a sheriff.

The vast majorities of big city police chiefs are not pro 2nd Amendment and function in an environment that attempts to limit private citizen's access to firearms. Police chiefs point toward violent crime to justify their position but there is a very different reality for them. A police chief is appointed by the city's political body and serves at the pleasure of that political body. The police chief may be supervised through a city manager, or mayor, but in reality the political body is the moving force behind hiring and firing of appointed positions. A council or board with a mayor are quite concerned with how voters in urban America respond to the issue of firearms and gun violence.

The vast majority of sheriffs are pro 2nd Amendment. Sheriffs are constitutional officers and are elected every four years. Their L.E. duties are normally in more rural areas and they tend to wish to keep their constituents happy, as many of these folks are very pro 2nd Amendment and frankly far less likely to be totally reliant on government.

To be fair minded, every now and again a big city police chief will see the light and come out as a gun rights advocate and draw the very logical conclusion that homeowners with guns are more likely to assist with crime reduction. This is even more relevant with the shrinking budgets L.E. has been faced with recently.

One such Police Chief is James Craig who has been the chief of police for the City of Detroit since 2012. Since Chief Craig began his tenure, the City of Detroit has seen a decline in violent crime such as homicide, robbery, sexual assault, and burglary. Chief Craig is quite candid in his position that firearms are just a small part of the solution for the City of Detroit but as he so saliently puts it "Guns aren't the only solution to Detroit's problems. But when the glass is heard smashing in the middle of the night, guns are among the most effective means of surviving a bad situation".[22]

It is a shame that more "big city" police chiefs do not receive the backing of their political bodies which would allow them to be a bit more forthcoming as it relates to firearms, police response to violent crimes, and self-reliance.

To illustrate the ridiculousness of politics with firearms look at the L.E. gun buyback programs that are meant to get firearms off the street by offering to pay cash to citizens who turn in their (or someone else's) firearms. In reality it is just a way for folks with nonfunctioning weapons to get some cash using local government as an overly generous pawnshop.

---

22   Craig, James. No Question in my Mind, Legal Gun Ownership Saves Lives. Jessica Chasman, The Washington Times. July 16, 2014.

The Politics of The Court System:

State Court System:

To further understand the decision to prosecute or not prosecute as it relates to self-defense a basic understanding of our court system is critical. State courts are comprised of a three tier system which is based on the federal court system. There are district courts, circuit courts, and appellate courts (which includes a state supreme court in most states). Judges preside over each court and are either elected or chosen by the general assembly in their respective states and jurisdictions. Generally there are two opposing sides in what we call an adversarial system of law. On one side is the prosecuting attorney who represents the state and locality. On the other side is the defense attorney who represents the accused.

It seems quite simple to this point. Not so fast; we have established that judges are elected or appointed which makes them beholden to the powers at the state level or to the voters in their city or county. Prosecuting attorneys are also political animals and in the vast majority of cases are elected and beholden to the voters in their respective jurisdiction.

To be fair, there is no perfect system for prosecutors and judges to be put into place. But, you can be sure that their political views reflect those who have put them into power. Which means in urban areas do not expect either to be pro firearms, or pro 2nd Amendment.

Federal Court System:

Federal courts are also comprised of this three tier system. We have already established that federal judges are appointed by the sitting president for life time terms. Though, in reality the president certainly will not be familiar with every person he appoints as a federal judge as there are 874 federal judge positions in the U.S. What occurs is a system called senatorial courtesy which simply means the president will take recommendations from members of congress with particular attention given to the party in power. As you can imagine this system can create cronyism where members of congress want like thinkers in these powerful positions.

Prosecuting attorneys at the federal level are called U.S. Attorneys and are appointed by the Attorney General to prosecute federal law and civil rights violations. The majority of these appointees at the upper levels will reflect the political leanings of the current presidential administration. These folks are part of the justice department, which is run by the Attorney General. The Attorney General is an appointed position as a member of the president's cabinet.

Hopefully the reader has not yet given up on reading based on a longwinded explanation of how and why the decision to prosecute may have been made. You can rest assured that any self-defense case that is a high profile one will get the attention of both local and federal authorities. The decision to prosecute is always based upon the facts of the case found during the investigation, but it also can be, and many times is, based upon politics.

What constitutes a "high profile" case? Well the reader can answer this question for themselves. Look to Trayvon Martin, Rodney King, and Mike Brown. Look to the Duke University Lacrosse team, and at professional athletes, and other public figures. And yes the elephant in the room is that many times there is a racial element involved. Considering the fact that there are many activists whose primary existence is to shed light on any and all potential civil rights violations make an already complex issue more complex. This will many times involve L.E., but private citizens who use force to defend are not immune to the highly charged political environment we live in.

> *"A man should look for what is, not what he thinks it should be".*
>
> **—Albert Einstein**

The Politics of The Police Response:

Police are not immune to politics in how they respond to civil disorder and public unrest. Nor are they immune in how they investigate "high profile" cases.

The standard police response to civil disorder can be quite political. Look at the L.A., California case involving Rodney King. Police chose to withdraw and/or not respond to certain areas in order to not appear heavy handed. This lack of response contributed to the truck driver, Reginald Denny, being pulled from his vehicle and severely beaten.

We can also refer to Ferguson, Missouri, where the shooting of Mike Brown occurred. Local police were overwhelmed and deferred to the state police whose biased agenda was based on the governor of the state. This certainly sent the message that looting and lawlessness was acceptable behavior.

While awaiting the politically and racially charged grand jury decision to indict or not indict the involved officer, it appeared that the governor was preparing to defend citizens and their property by deploying the Missouri National Guard.

What actually happened was that Governor Nixon, in favor of added security for government buildings, did not provide the needed security for the citizens of Ferguson. A change, many have charged, that may very well have ensured the burning of Ferguson.

It was reported that Missouri Lt. Gov. Peter Kinder accused the Obama administration of leaning on Nixon to withdraw the National Guard from the worst hit areas at the height of the unrest. At least a dozen burned businesses were described as "total losses" after the rioting, while many others were looted. Some store owners such as Mumtaz Lalani have reluctantly chosen not to rebuild and are planning to leave Ferguson altogether.[23]

A group called Oath Keepers, led by Sam Andrews, told the press that business owners in Ferguson were begging them to protect private property against violent protestors. Mr. Andrews had even accused the police of attempting to restrict his group's ability to provide security to property owners.

"Not only are they asking us to stay, more businesses are asking us 'do you have more men, can you guard our business

---

23   Kinder, Peter. Ferguson: Where was the National Guard? Brendan Keefe. USA Today, December 5, 2014.

too?' and so the business owners don't want us to leave," said Andrews, adding that residents believe the police have failed them in protecting against looters and arsonists.

This may only be property damage but in many cases it is the sole source of livelihood and income for these shop owners. Unfortunately some protestors, or street thugs, did not stop at property damage.

Case Study:

In St. Louis, Missouri, A 32-year-old man was beaten to death with hammers by at least two teens early Sunday morning on Itaska Street. The victim was identified as Zemir Begic, 32, of the 4200 block of Miami Street. He had injuries to his head, abdomen, face and mouth. He was taken to St. Louis University Medical Center, where he was pronounced dead.

Police said Begic was in his vehicle in the 4200 block of Itaska about 1:15 a.m. when several juveniles approached on foot and began damaging it. Begic got out and the juveniles began yelling at him and striking him with hammers. Two male juveniles, 16 and 15, were taken into custody.

Although it is impossible to know the clear reason for this attack it seems reasonable to assume it is related to the violent protests in nearby Ferguson. It is important to note that L.E. is not above choosing to not respond to civil unrest with acts of violence for the fear of appearing heavy handed, and to preserve the career of a politician or appointed official.

These thoughts are in no way meant to reflect poorly on law-enforcement, or the judiciary. Rather it is simply meant to illustrate how politically motivated many of the decisions are.

Even if you believe, as I do, that the vast majority of men and women in L.E. and the legal profession wish to do the right thing, we need to understand they are not the decision-makers for high-profile cases and high-profile issues. In fact, they never will be as this falls upon politicians and appointed officials.

There is no doubt that our system is still the best in the world but there are a number of folks in positions that have questionable agendas. Yes, there are checks and balances that should take care of this but they do not always work. To properly realize the complexities and differences in political views just look at how different laws relating to firearms are from state to state.

The old adage "better to be tried by 12 than carried by six" may be accurate, but I prefer "forewarned is forearmed". Any self-defense and/or firearms training you receive should not only have practicality in application but it also must include discussions on local, state, and federal law. It certainly would not hurt to discuss the local climate in self-defense particularly as it relates to deadly force for self-defense

New York City Police Commissioner Bill Bratton portrayed modern police as having "pent-up frustrations based on attacks by the federal government". Commissioner Bratton portrayed the populace as "being angry for many reasons which has caused people to take to the streets to protest. These protests have little to do with and go far beyond dissatisfaction with the police."[24]

Bill Bratton described this dissatisfaction as "being about the continuing poverty rates, the continuing growing disparity between the wealthy and the poor. It's still about unemployment

---

24 Bratton, Bill. Turning Backs on Mayor Inappropriate. SiLive.com.

issues. There are so many national issues that have to be addressed that it isn't just policing, as I think we all well know."

The Politics of the Media:

I would be remiss if I did not discuss the media. I am old enough to remember when both the printed and electronic media truly cared about finding and reporting the truth. Somehow the truth has become secondary and political agenda is the order of the day. The public's trust in government is at an all-time low; in fact, the only institution that the public trusts less than government is the media.

I was once a fan of the media. I grew up in a "newspaper" family. My grandfather, Alan Hathway, was the first managing editor of Newsday, a N.Y. daily paper. I can still remember how his investigative reporting put mob bosses in jail and the death threats he received because of it.

In fact, a well know story is told when he was approached by a man who asked him: "are you Alan Hathway"? When he said yes, the man knocked him to the ground with a punch. My grandfather got to his feet and said to the man "I am still Alan Hathway". These types of folks in the media no longer exist. All news revolves around the agendas of the owners of the individual media outlets.

We can watch, or read local news or national news and see the huge amount of press coverage involving workplace violence, and school violence and in particular school shootings. Guns are portrayed as a tool of violence as opposed to a tool to protect. Although there is a significant amount of anecdotal and statistical evidence, illustrating just how often firearms are used to protect, you seldom will see this type reporting on any news stations.

The Medias original intent was to focus on reporting the facts in order to assist the public in deciding the issue. What appears to be the primary focus of media now is to further social and political agendas. A perfect example is the case in Ferguson, Missouri where the fairy tale of Mr. Brown having his hands up and submitting to the police, but was still shot by the police, is perpetuated by the media even though there is no credible evidence to show this. Had the media just reported the facts, this fallacy would not have become accepted by so many based on media inaccuracy.

This issue is not only a problem in this country. In Britain the concern is that the media shapes public opinion too strongly, and that independent thought is not exercised. This is why the media in Britain is not allowed to report polling data until after elections. The relevance here illustrates that people believe what they read and hear from the media and either take action or take no action based on this oftentimes faulty information. The concern is that folks would either not vote or vote differently based on the media bias in reporting information.

When you compare this to high-profile cases like the one in Ferguson, Missouri and New York City you can see how inaccurate reporting portrayed circumstances that caused a significant public outcry where perhaps none was warranted.

The case in New York with Eric Garner was reported as police use of an "illegal chokehold". In fact the chokehold is not illegal, though it is against the agency policy. It reality it was not a chokehold at all, but a neck restraint.

The fear the reader should have is should they be forced to utilize a high level of force for defense, the facts may be inaccurately reported based on the media's desire to set a certain set of facts forward that further their social agenda The reader may be thinking that this will only occur if a law-enforcement officer is involved, though in reality this is no longer the case.

"A lie gets halfway around the world before the truth has a chance to get its pants on"
—Winston Churchill

Case Study (Warning Shot):

A Florida woman who claimed to be a victim of abuse yet was sentenced to 20 years behind bars for allegedly firing a warning shot during a dispute with her husband. She was granted a new trial. The appellate court ruling erased a decision by a jury that took just 12 minutes to convict Marissa Alexander, a mother of three, of aggravated assault.

Alexander unsuccessfully tried to invoke Florida's "Stand Your Ground" law as the same prosecutors who unsuccessfully worked to put Zimmerman behind bars told the court that she did not act in self-defense.

Alexander testified that, on Aug. 1, 2010, her then-husband, Rico Gray Sr., questioned her fidelity and the paternity of her 1-week-old child. She claimed that he broke through a bathroom door that she had locked and grabbed her by the neck. She said she tried to push past him but he shoved her into the door, sparking a struggle that felt like an "eternity."

Afterwards, she claimed that she ran to the garage and tried to leave but was unable to open the garage door, so she retrieved a gun, which she legally owned. Once inside, she claimed, her husband saw the gun and charged at her "in a rage" saying, "Bitch, I'll kill you." She said she raised the gun and fired a warning shot into the air because it was the "lesser of two evils."

The jury rejected the self-defense claim and Alexander was sentenced under the state's 10-20-life law, sparking outrage over how self-defense laws are applied in the state.

Alexander testified about three other alleged incidents of physical abuse by her husband, including one that led to his arrest. Several witnesses claimed to have seen the injuries she allegedly suffered and the final defense witness in the case testified that she met the criteria for "battered person's syndrome."

2nd Amendment Zealots:

There is plenty of fault to go around so I will spread the guilt. At the risk of offending some of our overzealous 2nd Amendment supporters, those who enjoy parading up-and-down in public with rifles and machine guns to make a point, I must submit they really do not help the cause. As I have told many police officers just because you can legally do something does not make it a good idea. Having zealots on both sides makes it difficult to have a reasonable discussion. The ultimate human right and ultimate human obligation should not be a political football, but unfortunately, it does seem to be such at times.

I can reflect back, as a police chief, to a town council meeting where I would be presenting a new town ordinance prohibiting discharging a firearm with-in the town limits except for self-defense. Based on the fact that our town had a population of 16,000 within six square miles, comprised of old carriage roads and homeowners, with ¼ acre lots and less, this seemed like a pretty good idea. The concern that anyone could walk outside and plink at cans or shoot garden pests with whatever ballistic round they chose was considered by most to be problematic.

Close to 100 2nd Amendment zealots showed up at the town council meeting, many armed, to contest this ordinance that would restrict their right to shoot indiscriminately within town limits. Only the most fanatical could construe this ordinance as a violation or threat to anyone's 2nd Amendment rights. Even though none of the 100 zealots were locals, the council allowed themselves to be intimidated and changed mid-stream in enacting the new ordinance.

"A fanatic is one who can't change his mind and won't change the subject"
—Winston Churchill

CHAPTER SIX

IT TAKES A VILLAGE:

The concept of "it takes a village to raise a child" is not one that I completely subscribe to. It is my belief that the raising of children is the sole purview of the parent. What I do advocate for is the concept of "it takes a village to keep a child safe". In fact, a better way to describe this is "it takes a village to keep the most vulnerable safe".

The ultimate human obligation is most critical when applied to those in our society who are the most vulnerable; which clearly includes children and the elderly (seniors). Although I do believe that women in some ways are more vulnerable than men, I believe that women fall more in the sheepdog role than that of the most vulnerable.

The Predator:

To understand why children and the elderly are the more vulnerable it is important to understand the make-up of a predator. When you study a predator in the wild scientists have found, and documented, a clear relationship between a predator and the slowest and weakest of a herd. This is done for the simple reason of self-preservation. If the predator expends too much energy unsuccessfully, or becomes injured they can no longer hunt and will starve

The human predator has very similar characteristics and tactics. A human predator is one who does not wish to work to earn their keep, and selects the weakest and most vulnerable as his prey. Human predators in many cases work in pairs or groups to ensure the odds are in their favor. The comparison between animal predators and human predators is a bit unfair to the animal. The animal predator does so out of hunger, whereas the human predator does so out of laziness and greed.

Although many studies have been completed in reference to the characteristics of a human predator my experience has shown that that they come in all shapes, sizes, backgrounds, and personalities. The only common traits are cowardice, and a sense of self entitlement.

Sexual Predator:

The sexual predator is a completely different animal than the predator who steals material goods and monies. The sexual predator is more violent and in most cases enjoys the actual physical domination of their victim. The sexual predator in many cases knows their intended victim, and in the case of children not only knows the child but spends significant time grooming the child. Most child sexual abusers target children whom they know and with whom they have established a relationship.

The grooming process occurs with abusers gaining access to their victims through deception and enticement, seldom using force. Abuse typically occurs during a long-term, ongoing relationship where the offender has established trust with their victim.

The Child Victim:

Ninety percent of child victims know their offender, with approximately half of the offenders being a family member. In the case of sexual assaults against adolescents aged 12 and older, approximately 80 percent of the victims know the offender.

Child victims may not be forthcoming and often do not tell for a variety of reasons such as shame, embarrassment, wanting to protect the offender, feelings for the offender, fear of being held responsible or being punished, fear of being disbelieved, and fear of losing the offender who may be very important to the child or the child's family.

Seniors as Victims:

Seniors are very vulnerable for a number of reasons. Crimes of violence against the elderly occur but it is more likely they will become victim to predators who prefer to use crimes of subterfuge and manipulation. There are many scams that are used to steal from the elderly that are successful because elderly have a desire to trust, are vulnerable, and need assistance.

The Bureau of Justice (BOJ) reports that between 2003 and 2013 3.6 per 1,000 seniors were victims of violent crime, and 72.3 per 1,000 seniors were victims of property crimes. BOJ statistics also show that only about 50% of seniors, who were crime victims, reported the crime to police. The BOJ also found that 59% of seniors who were victimized were in or near their home. Seniors are not only victimized by strangers, but by family and caretakers as well.

The types of fraud committed by strangers included: false prizes and sweepstakes; false investments; bogus charity contributions; home and automobile repairs where they were overcharged or the work was never completed; loans and mortgages at excessively high rates that change overtime; health, funeral, and life insurance; bogus health remedies; false travel expenditures; confidence games; telemarketing; and face-to-face contact.

The types of fraud committed by relatives and caregivers included: taking money; property, or valuables; borrowing money (sometimes repeatedly) and not paying it back; denying services or medical care to conserve funds; giving away or selling the elder's possessions without permission; signing or cashing pension or social security checks without permission; misusing ATM or credit cards, or using them without permission; doling out the elder's money to family or friends; and forcing the elder to part with resources or to sign over property

It clearly takes a village to protect those who are most vulnerable, family members cannot be present 24/7, and in some cases family and/or caretakers may be the abusers!

There are simple solutions that can
assist those who are most vulnerable:

- If you see a child alone, be aware of their surroundings. Is the child lost? Is the child being alone age appropriate? If anything does not seem right notify law-enforcement immediately.

- If an accompanied child appears highly uncomfortable, frightened, or overly subdued. Strike up a conversation with the adult accompanying the child. If anything does not seem right after this conversation notify law-enforcement immediately.

- Children are most vulnerable when they are alone.

- Develop relationships with the seniors in your neighborhood. Remember seniors are very proud, and in many cases will not ask questions in the fear of appearing ignorant on uninformed.

- If a senior feels comfortable around you they will bring up decisions they are making that may involve them getting scammed.

- If a senior in your neighborhood lives alone and has a caretaker, get to know the caretaker as well. Seniors are completely reliant on their caretakers and will be very reluctant to question anything the caretaker does.

- If something does not appear right in reference to how people are dealing with a senior, notify law-enforcement so they may investigate. Many L.E. agencies have experts in the field of fraud, white collar crime, and crimes against seniors.

As we discussed previously law-enforcement does an excellent job after the crime occurs with investigation and prosecution. Unfortunately, after the crime occurs making the victim whole is quite difficult. The damage, both financially and psychologically is seldom repaired.

In short, in order to be effective in exercising our ultimate human obligation we must be inquisitive, empathetic, and have developed relationships with neighbors. For these reasons I have always believed that women are natural protectors. Women are far better than men, they (as a general rule) are more willing to get involved when things do not seem right and do not worry about being embarrassed if things are different that they appeared. Women are natural protector, whereas men need more prompting at times.

This being said, it is still important to note that women are in certain cases more vulnerable than men. As a general rule women are smaller and not as physically strong as their male counterparts. Women are also targeted for different types of crimes than men are.

Another Frightening Case:
Nashville, Tenn. — A jury convicted two ex-Vanderbilt football players of raping a former student, rejecting claims that they were too drunk to know what they were doing and that a college culture of binge drinking and promiscuous sex should be blamed for the attack.

The victim, a 21-year-old neuroscience and economics major at the time of the June 2013 attack, cried as each guilty verdict was announced.

The jury heard two weeks of dramatic testimony from a parade of witnesses, including police, former and current Vanderbilt students and the woman, who said she didn't remember what happened that night, only that she woke up in a strange dorm room.

Vandenburg and Batey were on trial together, but represented by different attorneys. Attorneys for Vandenburg, who had been seeing the woman, said he did not assault her.

Testimony showed:

- Vandenburg passed out condoms to the other players, slapped her buttocks and said he couldn't have sex with the woman because he was high on cocaine.
- They also saw cellphone images from the night of the attack that Vandenburg sent to his friends as it was happening.
- Despite the photos and video, and witnesses seeing the woman unconscious and at least partially naked in a dorm hallway, no one reported it.
- The victim said in a statement she was hopeful the publicity from the case would lead to a discussion of how to end sexual violence on college campuses. In Nashville, where the prestigious private university is located, hundreds of college officials from across the state were meeting this week to discuss exactly that.
- "Finally, I want to remind other victims of sexual violence: You are not alone. You are not to blame," she said.

- Vandenburg's roommate at the time testified that he had been on the top bunk and saw the woman face down on the floor. He said he heard one of the players say he was going to have sex with her, but didn't do anything because he was afraid.

Defense lawyer's Argument:

Vandenburg and Batey were too drunk to know what they were doing and that a college culture of binge drinking and promiscuous sex should be partly to blame.

Deputy District Attorney Argument:

Tom Thurman told jurors that the college culture argument was a "red herring" and that the athletes thought the law didn't apply to them. "That's the culture that you really saw here," Thurman said. "Their mindset that they can get away with anything."

Rumors about what happened quickly spread around campus, and the assault might have gone unnoticed had the university not stumbled onto the closed-circuit TV images several days later in an unrelated attempt to learn who damaged a dormitory door. The images showed players carrying an unconscious woman into an elevator and down a hallway, taking compromising pictures of her and then dragging her into the room.

University Response:

School authorities contacted police, who found the digital trail of images. The university said after the verdict that they had kicked the players off the team many months ago, expelled them from school and were confident they acted appropriately.

"We will also continue our comprehensive ongoing efforts to raise awareness of the importance of every Vanderbilt student intervening when another student is at risk or in distress," the school said in a statement.

The Sobering Facts:

This case illustrates so many issues surrounding the ultimate human obligation being ignored by so many. These type actions are so despicable, lacking in a moral compass, and lacking in basic human empathy it is frightening.

The basics of this case involve a gang rape of an unconscious woman (who had been drugged), while bystanders watched and videotaped; during this incident not one person exercised their ultimate human obligation to stop the assault or at least report the assault.

These young men have illustrated all that is wrong with the culture of many sports teams, and fraternities. For this culture to be radically changed there must be actions taken at the highest levels of universities that illustrate a no tolerance policy of any predatory behavior.

As a retired L.E. who had been involved with investigating numerous violent crimes I can assure the reader this type predatory behavior does not manifest itself overnight. There must have been numerous smaller acts that went unpunished or ignored, and a culture of abuse must be present with that particular group.

The completely disingenuous defense that the defendants were "too drunk to know what they were doing and that a college culture of binge drinking and promiscuous sex should be blamed for the attack", really answers so many questions as to why these young men were willing to participate in a gang rape. Entitlement, because others were doing the same!

The fact that Vandenburg's roommate testified; "he had been on the top bunk and saw the woman face down on the floor. He said he heard one of the players say he was going to have sex with her, but didn't do anything because he was afraid", is again very telling.

The clear lack of empathy and lack of a moral compass is again, very frightening. A culture so strong that even non-participants to a violent gang rape are not willing to assist in any way show what a significant problem we have in our country, our universities, and even in our military.

In closing, if more of us would recognize our ultimate human obligation there would be far fewer victims than there currently are. This obligation requires us to spend more time getting to know our neighbors. This obligation requires us to take time out of our busy day to actively investigate when things do not appear correct and be willing to look silly on occasion if we have misinterpreted a situation.

I recollect back, as a young cop, to being dropped off in a neighborhood with the task of surveillance of a suspected drug house. In a very short time I was confronted by a home owner who thought my behavior was suspicious. It was! After identifying myself, the home owner went back inside his home.

In retrospect instead of being frustrated, I should have been very complimentary to the citizen who took his ultimate human obligation seriously.

In Early, Texas another citizen took this obligation seriously. Mr. Vic Stacy observed a police officer under fire in a trailer park where he resided.

The incident began when Charles Ronald Conner shot and killed two neighbors and their dogs in a quickly-escalating argument over excrement found on his property. Sgt. Steven Means of the Early Police Department responded to the bloody scene. Mr. Conner had hidden behind a tree and fired at the officer with an assault rifle as the officer arrived.

Sgt. Means took cover behind his police cruiser and returned fire using his own assault rifle. Neighbor, Vic Stacy stated that from inside his trailer, it appeared the officer might have difficulty getting a clear shot. Mr. Stacy stated to the Brownwood Bulletin "I thought 'he's fixin' to kill that boy.'"

Police estimate Stacy was about 150 feet away when he fired his .357 magnum pistol, striking Conner four times. Investigators determined as Conner returned fire to Stacy, Means also hit Conner at least twice, and a combination of their bullets killed him.

Police praised Stacy for his outstanding shooting in the incident, which happened July 29, and willingness to step in to a dangerous confrontation.

"The citizen that fired these shots did a tremendous job out there," Brown County Sheriff Bobby Grubbs said. "Had he not had a gun and the presence of mind to do this, we don't know what the outcome would've been".

In most cases there is only one opportunity to step in and stop a serious crime before it occurs. All of us do not have to be Vic Stacy. A simple recipe of getting to know our neighbors, taking a sincere interest in their well-being, and being aware of potential hazards to the most vulnerable is a huge step in the right direction. If we are too busy, unwilling to take the time, or unwilling to take the risk we allow the predators to win.

The Protectors:

The reader may remember that although I hold L.E. and the Judiciary in high esteem, I have been quite critical of both throughout this manuscript! I will now address another group whom I hold in the highest esteem.

I am a huge fan of our military, but in my black and white world there are no "sacred cows". I find the military an outstanding example to use to illustrate the Ultimate Human Right and Obligation! Our military is the best in the world, the best and brightest join our all-volunteer services. They go where we fear to go and protect us against all enemies foreign and domestic. No other group, other than law enforcement, should have a better understanding of the concepts I am discussing.

The Pentagon recently released new data about the reported number of sexual assaults in the military. Between July 1, 2012 and June 30, 2013 there were 3,553 reports of sexual assault, a 43% increase from the year before. During the same period, there were 219 casualties in the wars in Iraq and Afghanistan.

Last year, soldiers were 15 times more likely to be raped by a comrade then killed by an enemy.[25]

I truly believe the vast majority of men and women in the military are true heroes but it's impossible to ignore the elephant in the room when you see the epidemic of violence against women in our military. This can only be a reflection of the leadership and the culture within our military if the folks who are true heroes to the rest of their countrymen are preying upon their fellow heroes, not standing up for their fellow heroes, or ignoring the issue and allowing this culture to exist.

Just because an organization is an honorable one does not exempt them from scrutiny. In reality being a part of such an exceptional group with a tradition of honor and integrity brings with it the expectation of a higher standard. I do believe that our military is working hard to address this problem.

Leadership:

I will share with the reader my experience with training young men and women who are highly motivated and strong willed. To achieve any real change of a culture in an organization, you must get the first line leadership to buy in to the philosophy of the ultimate human obligation. If this does not occur you are just going through the motions, and the "training" will not take.

Young men have a tendency to be quite tribal and want to belong to a particular group that they are drawn to. Yes, the

---

25   Pentagon Study Finds 50% Increase in Reports of Military Sexual Assault. Helen Cooper. N.Y. Times, May 1, 2014.

military and Law Enforcement draw young men (and women) to the organization with a sense of belonging to something larger then what they are as an individual. On a smaller scale fraternities have this same draw. The groups that have a healthy outlook on how others should be treated do not allow disrespectful behavior or violence against others.

The informal leaders and first line supervisory personnel are who young people look to for mentorship and guidance. They can relate to and wish to emulate who they perceive as someone they would like to become one day. Senior leadership, in reality, can do very little to change the culture of an organization, particularly a large organization. Senior leadership must get the young leaders on board to the concept of the ultimate human obligation.

I would imagine that the ultimate human right is an easy sell, but the ultimate human obligation not so much.

This is what separates these organizations from a gang. This is why leadership in any organization or group is so critical. Followers will emulate their leaders; if leaders allow a culture of violence to exist then the ultimate human right and ultimate human obligation will pale in comparison to what image the leadership represents.

> *"The True Measure of Any Society can be found in how it treats its most vulnerable members"*
> —**Ghandi**

CHAPTER SEVEN

CONCLUSION

This final chapter is my last opportunity to truly sell you on the concept of the "Ultimate Human Right" and the "Ultimate Human Obligation". I believe that all of us need to become a champion for these concepts even if the reader believes in stricter gun control laws. These concepts are not mutually exclusive for those that are gun control advocates. I may not be one that believes in gun control but I have been to enough scenes of violent crime to understand the carnage that can be wreaked with a firearm, or any weapon, in the wrong person's hands.

The 2nd Amendment is just one portion of this manuscript. Regardless of your belief in gun ownership, there clearly should be no argument in relation to the ultimate human right of self-defense and the ultimate human obligation. I have certainly tried not to focus this entire manuscript on firearms but as Justice Anthony Scalia put so clearly "the handgun is Americans' preferred weapon of self-defense in part because it can be pointed at a burglar with one hand while the other hand dials the police."

Valid Concerns:

There has been and always will be a valid concern about firearms in the wrong hands. Laws that attempt to remedy this are not always bad. I am sure that the reader can agree that we do not want firearms in the hands of felons, the mentally ill, or those who are too young and immature to own one. Very few folks actually believe in gun ownership with no laws or regulations to govern their possession and use.

The USA leads the world in gun ownership, but it may actually be our culture that creates the higher number of mass shootings when compared to other countries where guns are prevalent. Statistics and studies have shown that those who commit Mass shootings, regardless of in what nation they occur, tend to be loners with not much social support who strike out at their communities, schools and families (Peter Squires, a researcher and professor, at the University of Brighton in the United Kingdom).[26]

Peter Squires found that:

---

26 Squires, Peter. In Europe, Fewer Mass Killings Due to Culture not Guns. Oren Dorrell, USA Today, December 18, 2012.

- Many other countries where gun ownership is high, such as Norway, Finland, Switzerland and Israel, tend to have more tight-knit societies where a strong social bond supports people through crises, and therefore mass killings are fewer.

- These other countries are: "In a sense they're less private" than in the USA, "but privacy and individualism is where some of the causes of crime and revenge are found".

- What stops crime above all are informal social controls. Close-knit societies where people are supported, where their mood swings are appreciated, where if someone starts to go off the rails it's noted, where you tend to intervene, where there's more support, all contribute to these social controls.

- Israel, where many men and women openly carry firearms while carrying out day-to-day activities, is a country where non-political mass killings are unheard of.

- Mass shootings have occurred in the past 20 years in Germany, Norway, Finland, Canada, Australia and the United Kingdom, but not as many as in the USA.

Any reasonable person must recognize that there are valid arguments on both sides of the debate. The clear winning argument, for me, is that our country was formed on a constitution and bill of rights. The 2nd Amendment and the ultimate human right and obligation trump all other arguments.

The Remedy:

It is quite clear that enacting laws that outlaw firearms is not the answer. Although many have argued for mandatory registering of firearms, and mandatory testing in order to own a firearm there are many reasons why this is not a viable answer.

The mandatory registering of firearms may sound reasonable, but is not manageable. It smacks of "big brother" and government overreach while putting the gun owners in jeopardy as targets of burglary and radical groups opposed to firearms. Laws such as "freedom of information" require government to share these type data bases with whoever wants them. Look no further than the "Journal News", a newspaper in New York that has received a wave of criticism from its readers after publishing the names and addresses of all of the individuals with handgun or pistol permits in its coverage area.

Hundreds of residents in New York's Westchester and Rockland counties were surprised to find their names and addresses listed on a map posted by The Journal News on Sunday. Users can click any dot on the map to see which of their neighbors has a permit for a gun.

Reporters such as Jo Craven McGinty, and two other New York Times reporters, sued for New York gun owners' addresses in 2010. The New York City Police Department gave them gun owners' names, but the NYPD argued against giving the gun owners addresses. Fortunately there was an exception that could be cited in the public records' laws of New York's open government law.

As for mandatory testing to legally own a firearm this is clearly a constitution issue. I have heard the argument that "you have to take a test to drive a car, why would you not have to take a test to own a firearm"?

There is a simplistic response to this argument. Gun ownership, similar to voting, is a constitutional right, driving is a privilege. In our very recent history: testing in order to vote and paying a poll tax in order to vote, was found to be a constitutional violation. Restrictions on our constitution rights are quite difficult to enact legislation for, and such laws seldom pass constitutional muster in federal court.

We should all be able to agree that self-defense is not always based on an equal playing field. At least half of our population, as a general rule, is smaller and weaker (physically) than the other half of the population. In writing about concepts relating to self-defense it would be negligent to ignore this fact. The ultimate human right should not be solely reliant upon size and strength, it must be a right held by all. The ultimate human right should not be based on the ability to pass a test, or pay a fee in order to own a firearm to defend one self. For this to be true, a mechanical advantage is critical.

I believe that the majority of us do not wish to spend inordinate amounts of time training just to be able to defend ourselves if the need may arise. Although I truly believe that not preparing yourself at all is very foolish I also believe that by over preparing, you can force your family into a life of fear and stress, which in many cases is worse than the actual event, should it occur. As Albert Einstein mentioned, we need to accept things as they are not as we think they should be. Clearly the world is a dangerous place; this may not be fair but it is accurate. To refuse to accept this fact just because you believe the world should not be this way, there should not be predators, and that you should not have to restrict your movement and the things you would like to do, is very foolish.

There are many worthy groups who advocate for self-defense education, training, and empowerment. I can't mention them all but there is one in particular that seems to be leading the way in self-defense education as a cornerstone for social change.

Rape Aggression Defense Systems (R.A.D.):

R.A.D. is considered by many as the national standard in self-defense education and training. R.A.D. is internationally recognized for programming quality and organizational commitment to excellence. R.A.D. Systems balances the needs of women to acquire self-defense education in a relatively short period of time, with the lifelong commitment required for physical skill mastery.

R.A.D. is the largest network of its kind with over 15,000 instructors receiving training. These instructors teach at various colleges, universities, and municipal law enforcement agencies as well as various other community organizations internationally. R.A.D. has trained more than 1,000,000 women since the program began in 1989.

R.A.D. is the only self-defense program ever endorsed by the International Association of Campus Law Enforcement Administrators (IACLEA), National Academy of Defense Education, the National Self- Defense Institute (NSDI), MACHO Martial Arts, and Redman Training Gear.

The R.A.D. Mission Statement is:
"The mission of the R.A.D. Systems is to establish an accessible, constantly improving and internationally respected alliance of dedicated Instructors. These Instructors in turn, will provide educational opportunities, available to everyone, in hopes they may create a safer future for themselves. In doing this, we challenge society to evolve into an existence where violence is not an acceptable part of daily life."

R.A.D. prides itself on being in the forefront of supporting the ultimate human right of self-defense and the ultimate human obligation of defending others. There are few, if any, other organizations the size and scope of R.A.D. who provide this type of training and support.[27]

Case Study (Sexual Assault on Campus):

We began with a case study discussing the sexual predator Jesse Matthew Jr. It would seem fitting to reexamine this case at the completion of this manuscript.

In 2002 Matthew was named as a suspect of a rape at Liberty University, the acclaimed Christian college, in Lynchburg, Virginia. Mr. Matthew was not arrested or charged but he was expelled. Liberty University would not say if and/or why Matthews was expelled.

According to Michael Doucette, the Commonwealth's Attorney for Lynchburg, Virginia, no charges were filed because the woman didn't want to go forward with the case and investigators determined there wasn't enough evidence to arrest Matthew.

---

27 Nadeau, Lawrence. WWW.rad-systems.com/.

According to a statement from Lynchburg police, a woman reported she was raped on the campus of Liberty University on October 17, 2002. Matthew told authorities that the woman consented, Doucette said, and added that there were no witnesses. The complaining witness in the case did not want to move forward with prosecution and there were no independent witnesses.

He transferred to Christopher Newport University, where he was a student from January 2003 through Oct. 15, 2003. He was a member of the football team from August 14 to Sept. 12, 2003. Mr. Matthew was again named as a suspect of a sexual assault and left the university for unknown reasons.

Police say suspect Jesse Matthew Jr. has links to both the recent disappearance of Hannah Graham and the 2009 murder of Morgan Harrington. Harrington's death has already been linked to a 2005 sexual assault in which the suspect was scared away. UVA student Hannah Graham is the fifth young woman in five years to vanish along the Route 29 corridor, and only one body has ever been found. The disappearances of an additional five young women from the area around Charlottesville, known as the Route 29 corridor, remain unexplained.

Morgan's Harrington's mother, who has tirelessly campaigned to bring her daughter's killer to justice states: "We worked five years to get to this point, so we are relieved."

The sad reality is these types of cases are not unusual. We may not always be there to prevent the attack or the assault and exercise our ultimate human obligation but we can certainly be there after the fact and provide every bit of support possible.

I may be idealistic, but I believe that in many cases the way we support and treat a person who has been hurt physically and emotionally, after the incident, may be more important than the incident itself. This is all part of the ultimate human obligation, not only taking action during an incident but our actions after the incident.

As a career L.E. officer who has investigated many violent crimes, when I see justification statements such as "the victim did not wish to move forward with the prosecution", and "there were no independent witnesses", I cringe. In many violent crimes, to include rape, there are no independent witnesses. In many cases you do not need one to move forward.

I immediately question how motivated this university was to provide the support all victims of violent crime need for them to be willing to endure the sheer hell of prosecuting their attacker in our court system. If the University, the Investigators, and the Prosecuting Attorney had been willing and sincere in their acceptance of the ultimate human obligation, perhaps the victim would have felt more comfortable moving forward with the prosecution.

If the victim had moved forward with the prosecution with full support of the University, the Investigators, and the Prosecuting Attorney perhaps we would not have between two and five other victims of Mr. Matthews.

Instead Mr. Matthews learned, what all violent predators learn after escaping a close call with potential jail and punishment, leave no witnesses!

Closing:

The ultimate obligation is required of each of us, based on our role, and abilities. Let's discuss taking action during an incident. Yes, not all of us are physically able to stop an attack. But.... we are all physically able to call for help (either yelling and/or dialing 911), and acting as a witness if needed. There is never an excuse not to at least do whatever part you are able in exercising our ultimate human obligation.

I was reading an old advertisement for martial arts instruction which used the term, "The manly art of self-defense". Well, self-defense and defense of others is no longer, and frankly never was, just manly. Looking to nature the greatest protectors of the young are females. Looking to humans the greatest protectors of small children are women. Being a protector seems to be a natural female trait regardless of the fact that women are normally not as strong, or large as men.

> *"I declare to you that woman must not depend upon the protection of man, but must be taught to protect herself, and there I take my stand".*
> **—Susan B. Anthony**

This said; it in no way absolves men of their part in relation to the ultimate human obligation. Frankly, if more people would believe in the ultimate human obligation and exercise this obligation the ultimate human right would be less necessary, and much simpler to accomplish. I truly believe that there are far more decent and good, than predatory people in the world and it is time for society to prove this by each of us stepping up and exercising our ultimate human obligation by becoming a guardian of necessity.

> *"For evil men to accomplish their purpose, it is only necessary that good men do nothing,"*
—**Rev. Charles F. Aked, Edmund Burke & John F. Kennedy**

About the Author:

Scott is a retired Law Enforcement officer with over 30 years of policing. Scott has served in every capacity from patrol officer to chief of police. Scott currently serves as the Deputy Director of the Hampton Roads Criminal Justice Training Academy in Virginia. He is a certified and current Firearms Instructor, Use of Force Instructor, and General Police Topics Instructor.

Scott also serves as the Director of Weapons Programming for R.A.D. Systems, based in Louisiana, and is the largest self-defense organization in the country. R.A.D. Systems has certified over 15,000 instructors and advocates for self-defense education as a cornerstone for social change.

Scott holds a Master's Degree in Government and Leadership Studies from Christopher Newport University, and serves as an adjunct instructor for Christopher Newport University in the Department of Social Sciences.

Scott has acted as an expert witness in the area of police use of force, police procedures and tactics, and civilian self-defense on numerous occasions.

Scott is married to Becky and has two grown children Jerry and Samantha. He and his wife live on the family horse farm in Preston, Maryland.

"You can be at ease only with those people to whom you can say any dam fool thing that comes into your head, knowing they will respond in kind, and knowing that any misunderstanding will be thrashed out right then, rather than buried deep and given a chance to fester".

—Travis McGee

Bibliography:

Beza, Theodore. "Christians, The 2nd Amendment ane The Duty of Self Defense." n.d.

Bratton, Bill. "Turning Backs on Mayer Inappropriate." *SiLive*, n.d.

Center, Pew Research. "Social and Demographic Trends Project." July 15, 2014.

Code, Brazilian Penal. *Abandonment of Children.* n.d.

Craig, James. "No Question in My Mind, Legal Gun Ownership Saves Lives." *The Washington Times*, July 16, 2014.

Darley, B. Latane & J. *Bystander Apathy.* 1969.

Dodson, Rober M. Yerkes & John D. "The Relation of Stress of Stimulus of Habit Formation." October 2004.

Hicks, William Edmund. *Hicks Law.* Wikipedia, n.d.

Jefferson, Thomas. *The Declaration of Independence.* n.d.

Juergensmeyer, Mark. *Islamic Views on Violence.* Wikipedia, n.d.

Kinder, Peter. "Ferguson: Where Was the National Guard?" *USA Today*, December 5, 2014.

Locke, John. *The Social Contract Theory.* n.d.

Madison, James. "The Federalist # 46." n.d.

Magna Carta or 1215. n.d.

Muzaffar, Chandra. "Interview on Frontline." n.d.

Nadeau, Lawerence. *WWW.rad-systems.com/.* n.d.

Puniyani, Ram. "Understanding Prophet Mohammad and Islam." n.d.

Quebec, Civil Code of. *Charter of Human Rights and Freedomes.* n.d.

Roland, A.L. Honig & J.E. "Shots Fired Officer Involved." *The Police Chief*, October 1998.

SCOTUS. *District of Columbia v. Heller.* SCOTUS U.S., n.d.

Spero, Aryeh. "Self Defense is a Religious Obligation." *American Thinker* (American Thinker), August 22, 2014.

Squires, Peter. "In Europe, Fewer Mass Killings Due to Culture Not Guns." *USA Today*, December 18, 2012.

Study, Pentagon. "Finds 50% Increse in reports of Military Sexual Assault." *N.Y. Times*, May 1, 2014.

Voigt, Cathryn A. Christy & Harrison. *Bystander Responses to Public Episodes of Child Abuse.* July 2006.

Wikipedia. *Athenian Military.* n.d.

—. *Good Smaritian Laws.* n.d.

Yantis, Steven. "Hopkins Study." *Force Science News*, August 1, 2005.